Fourth Edition

BUILDING YOUR CAREER

A GUIDE TO YOUR FUTURE

Susan Jones Sears
The Ohio State University

Virginia N. Gordon
The Ohio State University

Boston   Columbus   Indianapolis   New York   San Francisco   Upper Saddle River
Amsterdam   Cape Town   Dubai   London   Madrid   Milan   Munich   Paris   Montreal   Toronto
Delhi   Mexico City Sao Paulo   Sydney   Hong Kong   Seoul   Singapore   Taipei   Tokyo

Editor in Chief: Jodi McPherson
Acquisitions Editor: Sande Johnson
Editorial Assistant: Clara Ciminelli
Marketing Manager: Amy Judd
Project Manager: Susan Hannahs
Senior Art Director: Jayne Conte
Cover Designer: Bruce Kenselaar
Full-Service Project Management: Mohinder Singh / Aptara®, Inc.
Composition: Aptara®, Inc.
Printer/Bindery: Bind-Rite Graphics
Cover Printer: Lehigh/Phoenix
Text Font: Times

Credits and acknowledgments borrowed from other sources and reproduced, with permission, in this textbook appear on appropriate page within text.

Every effort has been made to provide accurate and current Internet information in this book. However, the Internet and information posted on it are constantly changing, so it is inevitable that some of the Internet addresses listed in this textbook will change.

Many of the designations by manufacturers and seller to distinguish their products are claimed as trademarks. Where those designations appear in this book, and the publisher was aware of a trademark claim, the designations have been printed in initial caps or all caps.

Library of Congress Cataloging-in-Publication Data
Sears, Susan Jones.
 Building your career : a guide to your future / Susan Jones Sears, Virginia N. Gordon. — 4th ed.
  p. cm.
 Includes bibliographical references and index.
 ISBN-13: 978-0-13-708452-4
 ISBN-10: 0-13-708452-8
1. Career development.   2. Vocational guidance.   3. College students—Employment. I. Gordon, Virginia N. II. Title.
 HF5381.S449 2011
 650.14—dc22   2010032699

10 9 8 7 6 5 4 3 2 1

www.pearsonhighered.com

ISBN 13: 978-0-13-708452-4
ISBN 10:   0-13-708452-8

To the memory of our loving mothers

Thelma L. Jones

Irma K. Niswonger

BRIEF CONTENTS

Chapter 1 AM I READY?   1

Chapter 2 WHAT DO I NEED TO KNOW ABOUT MYSELF?   10

Chapter 3 HOW DO I SEARCH FOR OCCUPATIONAL
INFORMATION?   26

Chapter 4 WHAT DO I NEED TO KNOW ABOUT EDUCATIONAL
ALTERNATIVES?   37

Chapter 5 HOW WILL I DECIDE?   54

Chapter 6 HOW CAN I PREPARE FOR THE FUTURE
WORKPLACE?   68

Chapter 7 HOW WILL I ADVANCE MY CAREER?   *THE JOB SEARCH
AND RÉSUMÉ WRITING*   77

Chapter 8 AM I THE BEST CANDIDATE?   *JOB LEADS AND THE JOB
INTERVIEW*   98

Chapter 9 WHERE DO I GO FROM HERE?   108

CONTENTS

Preface   xi

Chapter 1   AM I READY?   1

Why Do I Need to Plan?   2

1.1 Personal Factors   2

Why Do People Work?   3

1.2 My Concept of Work   3

How Do Educational Decisions Influence Career Choices?   4

1.3 How Decided Are You About a College Major?   4

What Are Some Barriers to Career Choice?   4

Other Barriers   5

1.4 Overcoming Barriers   5

Where Do I Start? The Career Choice Process   6

1.5 My Career-and Life-Planning Checklist   7

Case Studies: *Reflecting*   8

Summary Checklist   9

Chapter 2   WHAT DO I NEED TO KNOW ABOUT MYSELF?   10

My Personal Characteristics   11

Personality and Career Choices   11

Holland's Personality Types   11

2.1 Holland's Personality Types   11

Identifying My Interests   12

2.2 Assessing My Interests   12

Identifying My Values   14

2.3 Assessing My Work Values   15

Identifying My Skills   16

2.4 My Skill Profile   17

Summary Profile #1: My Personal Characteristics   19

How Does My Environment Influence My Career Choices   20

Socioeconomic Status (SES)   20

2.5 Exploring Socioeconomic Status   20

Family Influences   20

2.6 A Career Genogram   20

The Impact of Gender   23

2.7 What If?   23

Summary Profile #2: Environmental Influences on My Career Development and Choices   24

Pulling It All Together   24

2.8 Reviewing My Options   24

Case Studies: *Exploring*   25

Summary Checklist   25

Chapter 3   HOW DO I SEARCH FOR OCCUPATIONAL INFORMATION?   26

Starting My Search   27

3.1 What Occupations Interest Me?   27

3.2 Developing a List of Occupations to Search   28

Sources of Occupational Information   28

The Internet   28

O*NET   28

3.3 Using O*NET Online to Explore Occupations   29

Other Internet Resources   31

OCCUPATIONAL OUTLOOK HANDBOOK   31

CAREERONESTOP   31

USAJOBS   31

Career Guidance Systems   32

DISCOVER   32

FOCUS V.2   32

SIGI 3   32

Direct Experience   32

Informational Interviews   32

3.4 Conducting an Informational Interview   33

Narrowing Down My Choices   35

Case Studies: *Exploring*   36

Summary Checklist   36

Chapter 4   WHAT DO I NEED TO KNOW ABOUT EDUCATIONAL ALTERNATIVES?   37

Choosing an Educational Direction   37

4.1 What Type of Education Do I Need?   38

Why Attend College?   39

4.2 Why Am I in College?   39

Making Initial Decisions   39

The Undergraduate Curriculum   40

Choosing a Major   41

4.3 Exploring Majors   42

4.4 Researching a Major   46

Graduate or Professional Education   48

Distance Learning   51

Experiential Learning   51

EXTRACURRICULAR ACTIVITIES   51

WORK EXPERIENCES   51

INTERNSHIPS AND COOPERATIVE EDUCATION   51

STUDY ABROAD   52

VOLUNTEER WORK   52

SERVICE LEARNING   52

Case Studies: *Exploring*   53

Summary Checklist   53

Chapter 5   HOW WILL I DECIDE?   54

Factors in Decision Making   55

5.1 How I Make Decisions   55

Dimensions of Decision Making   56

Myself as Decision Maker   56

5.2 Identifying My Values   56

5.3 Using My Career Values in Decision Making   57

Risk Taking   57

5.4 Am I a Risk Taker?   57

Personal Decision-Making Style   58

5.5 My Decision-Making Style   59

The Decision Situation   59

CHANGE   60

INDECISION   60

OBSTACLES   60

5.6 Checklist of Obstacles   60

CONTROL   61

The Decision-Making Process   61

DEFINING THE PROBLEM   61

STATING YOUR GOALS   61

5.7 What Are My Goals?   63

COLLECTING INFORMATION   63

LISTING ALTERNATIVE SOLUTIONS   63

5.8 Identifying Alternatives   64

CHOOSING ONE OF THE ALTERNATIVES   64

5.9 Why Some People Don't Act on Their Decisions   65

Taking Action on My Choice   65

5.10 Action Plan   65

REVIEWING YOUR CHOICE PERIODICALLY   66

5.11 Making Decisions   66

Case Studies: *Deciding*   67

Summary Checklist   67

Chapter 6   HOW CAN I PREPARE FOR THE FUTURE WORKPLACE?   68

What Factors Are Influencing the Present and Future Workplace?   69

6.1 You and the Future Workplace   69

What Do I Know About the Workplace and Hiring Trends for the Next 5 to 10 Years?   70

Workforce Trends   70

Employment Projections   71

6.2 Searching for Job Outlook and Projection Data   73

How Can I Prepare for the Future Workplace?   74

Career and Life Skills   74

6.3 How Ready Am I?   74

Case Studies: *Preparing*   76

Summary Checklist   76

Chapter 7   HOW WILL I ADVANCE MY CAREER?   *THE JOB SEARCH AND RÉSUMÉ WRITING*   77

Selling Myself   77

Taking Action Steps   78

Writing a Résumé   79

Résumé Formats   80

Common Résumé Errors   80

Appearance   81

Final Touches   82

Résumé Dissemination   82

Video Résumés   82

Electronic Résumés   82

Scannable Résumés   82

Maintaining a Résumé File   83

7.1 Sample Résumé Worksheet   83

7.2 Résumé Worksheet   86

Writing a Cover Letter   94

Case Studies: *Preparing*   97

Summary Checklist   97

Chapter 8   AM I THE BEST CANDIDATE?   *JOB LEADS AND THE JOB INTERVIEW*   98

Generating Job Leads   98

Job Search Sources   99

NETWORKING   99

NEWSPAPERS   99

EMPLOYMENT SERVICES   99

JOB FAIRS   100

FRIENDS AND FAMILY   100

DIRECT CONTACTS   100

Career Mentors   100

Job Searching on the Internet   100

Job Interviewing   101

Preparing for the Interview   101

During the Interview   102

INTERVIEW FORMATS   103

CYBER-INTERVIEWS   104

APPEARANCE   104

ETIQUETTE   104

After the Interview   104

8.1 Interview Follow-Up   104

Legal and Illegal Inquiries   105

Dealing with Rejection   105

8.2 Handling Rejection   106

Job Search Review   106

Case Studies: *Preparing*   107

Summary Checklist   107

Chapter 9   WHERE DO I GO FROM HERE?   108

9.1 Method 1: A Snapshot in the Career-Planning Process   108

9.2 Method 2: Evaluating Your Career Planning   108

9.3 Method 3: My Career and Life-Planning Checklist Revisited   109

9.4 Action Planning   112

Case Studies: *Jed and Maria*   112

Case Study: *Me*   113

References   115

Index   117

PREFACE

Building a career is a lifelong process requiring a broad base of knowledge and skills. Individuals will draw upon this career knowledge and their decision-making skills many times during their lifetime as they explore, work in, and change career fields. Although some individuals are deliberately and continually involved in their career planning, many others make career decisions only as the need arises—or even allow circumstances to dictate their career paths, sometimes with less than satisfactory results.

Today's workplace is undergoing dramatic changes. To prepare for the future workplace requires a new perspective on where, how, and why people work. Many new and different personal qualities and attitudes and much workplace knowledge will be required in addition to the expertise and skills needed to perform specific jobs. Lifelong learning will be an essential part of every worker's life.

The intent of this book is to help students and others who are searching for a career direction to learn how to explore, assimilate, and use personal and occupational information so they can make satisfying career decisions now and in the future. Once they understand and practice the career decision-making process, they will be able to competently manage their careers.

New in this fourth edition are many reorganized and updated chapters to help the career decision maker experience the important tasks involved in building a career. Chapter One introduces readers to the important factors involved in understanding their own attitudes and feelings toward work and how they personally might engage in the career planning process. A model for understanding the different phases involved in this process is presented, and each chapter offers exercises and information to help the reader become involved. While the career choice process is sequential in this book, the process experienced by real people never is easy or linear. The intent of this book is to offer insights into the elements involved and the opportunity to acquire solid personal, educational, and occupational information on which to base satisfying and realistic decisions at every stage of life.

Assessing the personal characteristics in Chapter Two (on personality, interests, values, and skills) has been reframed within the U.S. Department of Labor's O*NET system. The important environmental influences affecting career choices have also been updated. The occupational information searches in Chapter Three has been reconfigured so the reader can experience the search process firsthand. Occupations that have been suggested by the self-assessment results in Chapter Two can be researched on the Internet and through other viable sources.

Chapter Four examines various educational options and college curricula. A matrix relates more than a hundred college majors to the self-assessment results in Chapter Two. Chapter Five pulls together within a decision-making framework the elements researched in previous chapters. Readers examine many aspects of how they make decisions, including their own decision-making style. They are actually encouraged to make a decision about a major or occupation, even if it is tentative. Another aspect of this new edition is an emphasis in Chapter Six on the need to prepare for the future workplace. Readers learn about the changing workplace, the personal qualities necessary for success. They also explore additional information about occupations by searching employment projections and job outlooks.

Chapters Seven and Eight are updated to provide the reader with tips on how to write a résumé and the many factors related to mounting a job search. Stressed is the importance of beginning this important aspect of career planning early in the college years and not waiting until it is time to graduate. Chapter Nine, the last chapter, helps readers pinpoint where they are in the career decision-making process and offers three methods for summarizing the knowledge and skills they have acquired throughout this journey. It also emphasizes the importance of continuing to use the career planning knowledge and skills they have acquired. The lessons learned through the content and exercises readers experience in this book will help them understand how to make realistic and satisfying career decision now and in the future.

ACKNOWLEDGMENTS

We would like to thank all the students who, in using various editions of this book, offered us valuable feedback about their diverse career planning needs, as well as the course instructors who have made helpful suggestions. We would like to acknowledge Dr. Margie Bogenschutz, who offered her expertise for the job-search part of this book. The following reviewers provided input on improvements for this fourth edition: Dr. Christie Rinck, University of South Florida, and Susan Loffedro, Northeastern University.

CHAPTER 1

Am I Ready?

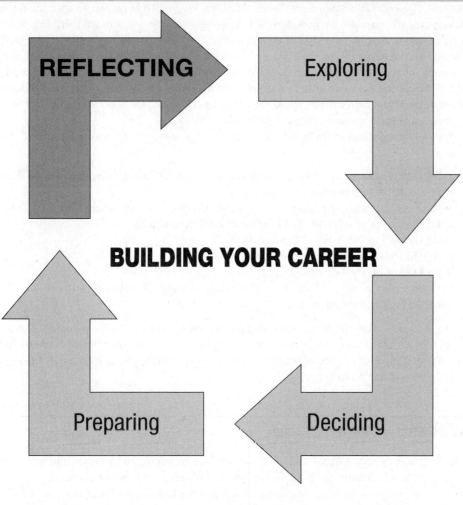

REFLECTING   Exploring

BUILDING YOUR CAREER

Preparing   Deciding

*"Choose a job you love and you will never have to work
a day in your life."*

CONFUCIUS

Is there a magic formula for choosing a career? What are the factors involved? Some career theorists think personal qualities, such as our interests and aptitudes or what we value, are the key factors in the process. An older theory that many still hold true is that you need to match these personal characteristics to compatible work environments in order to be happy with your work. Other theorists think our family and socioeconomic background and even our heredity greatly influence career choices. Still others think our perceptions of who we are, or our self-concept, influences the occupational alternatives we consider.

One widely accepted theory is that choosing a career is part of our overall development as individuals. The developmental approach takes into account the different stages we pass through from childhood to mature adult. The career development process, therefore, includes choosing, entering, adjusting to, and advancing in a series of career choices. Studies suggest that most people will hold six to nine jobs during their lifetime. In today's world, you will probably follow an ongoing career path that will involve many career decisions along the way. That is why, you need to learn about the career planning process now, so you are prepared to meet the challenges of our rapidly changing work place.

WHY DO I NEED TO PLAN?

As noted, the career planning process begins early in life and continues throughout your lifetime. The extent of parental encouragement you received, the kind of toys you played with, the myriad of experiences you engaged in, and the role models you were exposed to have influenced your perceptions of yourself and the kind of person you want to become. As you grew up, you probably created certain occupational fantasies; for example, you may have wanted to be a rock star, a professional tennis player, or an astronaut. As you got older and knew yourself better, you had additional ideas, perhaps more closely related to the reality of who you are. Your early fantasies, however, often reveal many truths about the kind of person you are now. Those fantasies offer clues about your basic interests, values, and abilities.

As you thought about different career choices, you might have asked some of these questions:

- What kind of occupations have I considered in the past? What attracted me to those fields? How are they different from my current ideas?
- What do I want in my work (e.g., to make a lot of money, to work where I can use my technology interests, to work where I can find mental stimulation)?
- What should I major in when I'm in college?
- How will I know if my career decisions are good?
- What kind of lifestyle do I want?
- Do I have what it takes to be a success? What does being successful mean to me?
- What do I really want out of life?

These are just a few of the basic questions that are involved in career and life planning. Although we do not have total control over every facet of our lives, we *can* increase our odds of obtaining a satisfying and productive career through ongoing and careful planning. Exercise 1.1 asks you to evaluate your readiness to begin this important process.

EXERCISE 1.1   Personal Factors

Certain personal factors will affect how ready you are to begin the career planning process. Evaluate how the following personal factors might influence your readiness to engage in the exploration and decision-making tasks contained in this book. Mark the place along each continuum where you think you are today.

Motivation. How motivated are you to spend the considerable time and energy required to be involved in the process of career planning?

Not Very Motivated	*Somewhat Motivated*	*Highly Motivated*

Responsibility. How able are you to take full responsibility for your involvement in the career-planning process and in your decisions, regardless of outcome?

Not Very Responsible	*Somewhat Responsible*	*Highly Responsible*

Compromise. How willing are you to examine (and possibly change) a strongly held belief or decision if it seems to be unrealistic or unattainable when new information indicates that a compromise is necessary?

| *Compromise Sometimes* | *Difficult Sometimes* | *Compromise Easily* |

Commitment. How able are you to commit to a decision once you are convinced it is the best one at the time?

| *Commit Sometimes* | *Difficult Sometimes* | *Highly Committed* |

Do you anticipate any problems associated with the personal factors above? Which ones, and how might they influence your career planning progress?

_____

_____

_____

_____

What other personal factors or attitudes might influence your readiness to begin the career planning process?

_____

_____

_____

_____

WHY DO PEOPLE WORK?

Have you ever wondered why people work? On the surface the reason seems obvious—to make a living—but there are other important reasons as well. Some people work for status, for the opportunity to be creative, or for the relationships work provides. Many people find their sense of identity through their work.

Attitudes toward work have a great impact on our aspirations and how we plan our lives. The quotes in Exercise 1.2 indicate the broad range of people's perceptions of work. They reflect philosophical, psychological, practical, and even negative views of work.

EXERCISE 1.2   My Concept of Work

Check three quotes below that best express *your* concept of work:

_____ "Real success is finding your lifework in the work that you love."   *David McCullough*

_____ "It has been my experience that one cannot, in any shape or form, depend on human relations for lasting reward. It is only work that truly satisfies."   *Betty Davis*

_____ "All paid jobs absorb and degrade the mind."   *Aristotle*

_____ "Do not hire a man who does your work for money, but him who does it for love of it."   *Henry David Thoreau*

_____ "Work is a four-letter word."   *Unknown*

_____ "Nothing is really work unless you would rather be doing something else."   *James M. Barrie*

_____ "People who work sitting down get paid more than people who work standing up."   *Ogden Nash*

_____ "A working person is a happy person."   *Unknown*

_____ "You can take this job and shove it—I ain't workin' here no more."   *Popular song*

_____ "Work is love made visible."   *Kahlil Gibran*

Write your personal concept of work.

_____

_____

How will your view of work affect the way you engage in the career planning process (e.g., money isn't important if I can do the work I love; I need to find a career that won't bore me to death)?

_____

_____

HOW DO EDUCATIONAL DECISIONS INFLUENCE CAREER CHOICES?

A critical component of the career planning process is making educational or academic decisions. If you are already committed to a college major, your occupational exploration may appear to be confined to that general area. This is not necessarily true since any major can lead to many jobs. If you are still undecided about an academic direction, this book will help you narrow down your possibilities. Exercises 1.3 and 1.4 will help you think about where you are in making an educational decision.

EXERCISE 1.3   How Decided Are You About a College Major?

/_____/_____/_____/_____/_____/_____/

Very decided   Somewhat decided   Undecided

If you are *very decided*, what major have you chosen? What attracted you to this major?

_____

_____

If you are *somewhat decided*, what do you need in order to commit to this major (e.g., more occupational information; the coursework involved; my ability to succeed in it)?

_____

_____

If you are *undecided,* what majors have you considered? Why?

_____

_____

What do you need to help you decide on a major (e.g., more information about my interests and abilities; more information about the jobs I can get with it; afraid I'll make the wrong decision)?

_____

_____

In Chapter Four you will explore many academic alternatives and how these majors relate to personal characteristics and occupational fields. In this way, you will be able to see the possible relationships between your educational and career choices.

WHAT ARE SOME BARRIERS TO CAREER CHOICE?

Some beliefs about careers prevail in our culture, and certain attitudes, thus, are perpetuated. Examine these career beliefs:

There is a perfect job for me if I can just find it.

I can do any job that interests me as long as I am motivated and put forth the effort.

Educational and vocational choices are the same.

Most people wouldn't work if they didn't have to.

Most people dislike their work.

The younger people are when they choose a career, the better off they are.

People know when they've chosen the right work because the job is fun.

Certain jobs are best suited for men and certain jobs are best suited for women.

Others know more about me than I do, so they will make a better career choice for me.

Choosing an occupation is a once-in-a-lifetime decision, so it should be the right one.

Although a few of these statements possibly contain a kernel of truth, most experts agree that these statements are essentially false. In fact, some of these beliefs are unrealistic and may impede your progress through the career-planning process. Check out your beliefs and ask yourself, "Will any of my beliefs prevent me from taking certain courses of action or considering certain occupational areas?" If so, discuss your beliefs with your instructor, classmates, friends, and family.

OTHER BARRIERS

Other barriers can prevent you from making satisfying and timely career choices. Here are a few that could impede your career exploration.

- *You may feel pressured to make a specific academic or occupational choice that family members, peers, or other important people in your life want you to make.* If you agree with this choice, there is no problem. If you have different ideas about your interests and what is important to you, you should pursue these alternatives by actively gathering information about them. In this way, you'll have choices to compare with the original idea and later won't regret not having explored them.
- *You may not be ready to make a career decision because of procrastination, lack of motivation, apathy, laziness, or a preoccupation with important events in your life.* Career exploration and planning take place over a lifetime. You have been doing it since you were a child and usually are engaged in some facet of the process regardless of whether you are aware of it. Although you may not be "ready," you can gather information for future reference anytime and anywhere. For example, you might talk to upper-class students and faculty about majors or to workers in specific jobs. Work and volunteer experiences also are useful sources of career information. Personal behaviors and traits such as procrastination and lack of motivation may be habits that require examination in other contexts as well as in career planning.
- *You may not know how or where to begin the career exploration process.* Because we think about our future throughout our lives, it is natural to continue to collect, weigh, and absorb information that we can use eventually in the career decision-making process. Consulting with a career counselor or an academic adviser may be a place to begin if this seems like a barrier to taking action.
- *You might be so anxious and overwhelmed with the prospect of beginning a search that you do nothing.* If you are experiencing extreme anxiety when making academic or occupational choices, it may be helpful to consult a counselor. This is especially true if you have difficulty making decisions about other aspects of your life as well. In Exercise 1.4, you are to consider barriers to career planning on a personal level.

EXERCISE 1.4   Overcoming Barriers

What specific barriers do you think might affect *your* progress in career exploration and decision making (e.g., lack of information, lack of motivation, not knowing where to begin)?

_____

_____

_____

What can you do to overcome these barriers now? In the future?

_____

_____

_____

WHERE DO I START? THE CAREER CHOICE PROCESS

Since every person has unique personal characteristics, matures at a different pace, and lives in a specific environment, career decision making becomes an individual life journey. The type of work that interested you at age 18 may be quite different from your interests at age 25 or 40. Every day, scores of people change careers. The need to be open-minded and flexible, therefore, is critical to negotiating your career journey. This book will help you experience the career decision-making process, as shown in Figure 1.1 and will help you understand the critical factors in making satisfying educational and occupational choices.

Although most people move consciously or subconsciously through these phases, they travel at different speeds and levels of understanding. *Each of us will negotiate the process differently and not always in the same order.* You may be ready for the *Exploration* phase, for example, while another student may already be in the *Deciding* phase. Other students may need to return from the *Deciding* phase to *Exploring* because the choices they made proved to be unrealistic. Still others might be stymied in the *Preparing* phase because they skipped the *Exploration* and *Deciding* phases entirely.

Chapter One is just the beginning of understanding what the career-planning process is all about. In Chapter Two you will gather information about your interests, strengths, and other critical personal information. In Chapter Three you will use this personal information to explore occupational fields that might interest you. Chapter Four will help you explore academic possibilities. Chapter Five will help you examine the way you make decisions in general and will specifically guide you through the decision-making process. Chapter Six offers a picture of tomorrow's workplace and what personal qualities you will need to be successful there. Chapters Seven and Eight will help you refine your job-search skills, and in Chapter Nine you will review what you have learned and establish long-term goals. Exercise 1.5 will begin to familiarize you with the tasks involved in each step of the career planning process.

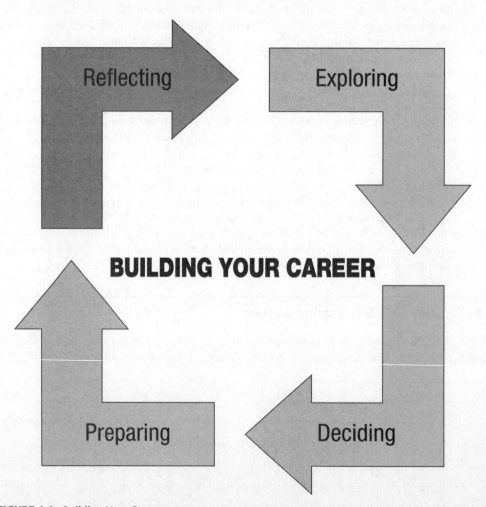

FIGURE 1.1 Building Your Career.

EXERCISE 1.5   My Career- and Life-Planning Checklist

This Career- and Life-Planning Checklist will give you a preview of what you can expect to learn about the tasks involved in each step of the career planning process. Think about the knowledge, skills, attitudes, and behaviors you will need in order to make educational and career decisions. The items are organized according to the tasks outlined in Figure 1.1: Building Your Career. *Check those items that you need or want to learn as you progress through each chapter.* At the conclusion of this book, you will check these items again (Exercise 9.3) to determine what you have learned as well as what you still need or want to know.

hi
Josey

Chapter One: Am I Ready?

_____ What is involved in career and life planning? Where am I currently in this process?

✓ Am I ready to take the time and responsibility **now** to actively engage in career planning?

_____ How might my perception of "work" influence my career choices?

Chapter Two: What Do I Need to Know About Myself?

✓ How might my personality influence my occupational choices?

✓ What are my occupational interests?

✓ What do I value in a job (e.g., income, co-workers, self-employment)?

✓ What are my current skills, and what new ones do I need to learn?

✓ How might my family background affect my career choices?

✓ How might my gender influence my career choices?

Chapter Three: How Do I Search for Occupational Information?

_____ How do I find occupations that are realistic for me to explore?

_____ How can I compare my interests, values, and skills to certain occupational alternatives?

_____ Where can I find important information abut specific occupations (e.g., salaries, required skills, educational requirements, employment trends)?

_____ What are the best sources for finding occupational information (e.g., Internet, printed, electronic, personal interviews)?

_____ What experiences will help me test my ideas about an occupational field (e.g., internships, volunteer work, study abroad)?

_____ How can I evaluate and use occupational information once I have found it?

Chapter Four: What Do I Need to Know About Educational Alternatives?

_____ How do certain majors match my academic strengths?

_____ How can I find information about specific majors (e.g., talk to faculty, academic advisors, seniors in major, alumni)?

_____ What occupational fields relate to the college major(s) I am considering/pursuing?

_____ What type of education will I need to enter certain occupations (e.g., two- or four-year degree, technical degree, graduate or professional study)?

_____ How can I identify the courses that will strengthen the knowledge and skills I will need for certain jobs?

Chapter Five: How Will I Decide?

_____ Why is understanding my personal style of making decisions important?

_____ How can I learn to become a more effective career decision maker?

_____ How can I be more effective and realistic in setting short- and long-term goals?

_____ How do I put into action an educational and/or career decision I have made?

_____ Why is reevaluating career decisions periodically so important?

Chapter Six: How Can I Prepare for the Future Workplace?

_____ What are the factors that are influencing the present and future workplace?

_____ What are the workforce and hiring trends for the next 5 to 10 years?

_____ How can I search for information about the job outlook for the occupational fields I am considering?

_____ What qualities will employers value in the future workplace, and how can I begin to make myself more marketable?

Chapter Seven: How Will I Advance My Career? The Job Search and Résumé Writing

_____ What job-search skills do I need to learn?

_____ What are the qualities of an effective résumé?

_____ What are the essentials in writing a good cover letter?

_____ What do I need to know about technology and other methods to search for a job?

Chapter Eight: Am I the Best Candidate? Job Leads and the Job Interview

_____ How can I generate job leads?

_____ What is the best way to prepare for a job interview?

_____ What is good interviewing behavior?

_____ Where can I learn about cyber-interviews and other electronic methods?

_____ What does an interview follow-up entail?

Chapter Nine: Where Do I Go from Here?

_____ Where am I now in the career decision-making process?

_____ What action steps do I need to take to continue my career planning?

At the end of this book, you will find another copy of this checklist. At that time you will be able to determine what career planning knowledge you have acquired and what career and academic planning tasks you may still need to accomplish.

CASE STUDIES

Reflecting

JED

Jed is a first-year student at a moderately large college. He knows that eventually he will need to make a decision about a major, but doesn't feel strongly about any field. He feels frustrated, as he senses that his parents want him to make firm academic and career decisions soon. They have encouraged him to think about engineering because he seems to have a talent for math and science. Jed doesn't know much about engineering and is not sure he has the ability or motivation to pursue the difficult curriculum in this area.

His academic advisor has encouraged him to take a career course that is being offered, and Jed has agreed. He hopes that by exploring different career fields in an organized, systematic way, he will discover what might be compatible with his interests and abilities.

MARIA

Maria has worked as a secretary in a high-tech firm since graduating from high school. Even though she completed a college preparatory track in high school, she didn't go on to college because she thought it would be too much of a financial drain on her family. No one else had gone to college in her family, and it seemed like a difficult goal to attain.

As a worker, Maria has been quite successful. Fortunately, she has a competent supervisor who was quick to recognize her skills. Even though most of Maria's duties remain clerical, she has been encouraged to expand the scope of her work. She has discovered that she is quite good with computers. She is able to spend a couple of hours a day working alongside a computer programmer and is learning programming language. Her company has a college tuition reimbursement program that she has decided to explore.

Maria was divorced recently and is highly interested in improving her earning capacity so she will be able to take care of her young daughter. Maria has decided to take a career-planning course at her local community college to help her gather information and focus on making a timely decision. ■

Summary Checklist

WHAT I HAVE LEARNED

____ The career planning process began in my childhood, and I will continue to make career decisions the rest of my life.

____ I need to be ready to commit a great deal of time and effort to this important work.

____ It is important to identify my personal attitudes and beliefs about work since they can affect how I will approach the career planning process and the choices I make.

____ The items I checked on the Career and Life Planning Checklist will guide me as I set goals and progress through this course.

HOW I CAN USE IT

I feel confident that by engaging in the process outlined in this text, I will be able to make educational and/or career decisions that will be realistic and satisfying *for this time in my life.*

The next step: If you are using this book in a course, you will have the opportunity to discuss all aspects of the career-planning process with your instructor and other students. If you are using this book for self-study, obtaining the services of a career counselor can be invaluable. Regardless, you are the one who needs to take full responsibility for "building your career." *You are the one who will live it!*

CHAPTER 2

What Do I Need to Know About Myself?

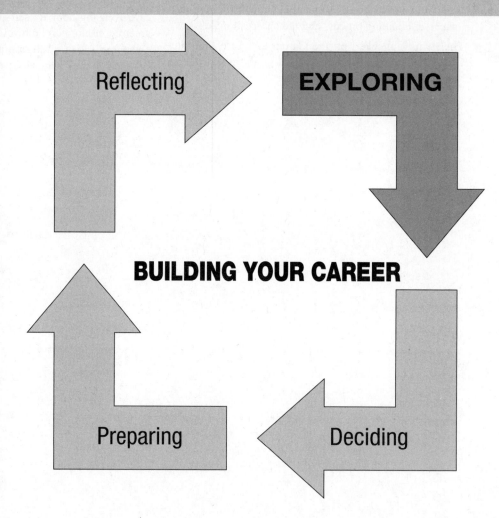

"Hide not your talents. They for use were made. What's a sundial in the shade?"

BENJAMIN FRANKLIN

As you learned in Chapter One, career development and planning constitute a process that includes reflecting, exploring, deciding, and preparing for the workplace. In this chapter, you begin to explore by gathering information about yourself. You will:

- identify your personality traits and interests,
- identify key values,
- reflect upon your skills, and
- consider influences in your environment, such as socioeconomic class, family patterns, and gender.

MY PERSONAL CHARACTERISTICS

Personality and Career Choices

Personality is a collection of qualities or traits that are somewhat stable across situations. These qualities play an important role in your career decision making. Your personality emerges in both home and work environments. For example, if you are outgoing and assertive with your friends, you probably will be outgoing and assertive with your colleagues at work. However, if you are forced or encouraged to tone down your natural personality at work, then you may be unhappy or feel that you don't fit in that job.

Although personality is important to consider as you make career choices, keep in mind that most occupations accommodate a variety of personality characteristics. Certain personality traits are, however, critical to success in some occupations. A naturally gregarious and persuasive person may be more successful as a politician or sales representative than a quiet, shy person, whereas a warm and empathic person may be more successful as a professional counselor than a person who is reserved and doesn't feel comfortable expressing feelings.

Holland's Personality Types

John Holland, a career theorist, has studied personality and work environments and suggests that your personality is reflected in the type of occupational environments or workplaces you choose. Holland theorizes that your personality is a product of both your heredity and your experiences and that these, in turn, influence your preferences for a variety of activities and tasks. Holland believes that your choice of an occupation is an expression of your personality and that members of an occupational group have similar personalities. He also maintains that occupational achievement, stability, and satisfaction depend on congruence between personality and a person's chosen work environment (Holland, 1997). Exercise 2.1 will help you discover how Holland's personality types might relate to you.

EXERCISE 2.1   Holland's Personality Types

Holland suggests that most persons can be categorized as one of six personality types: Realistic, Investigative, Artistic, Social, Enterprising, or Conventional. Another way of thinking about each of the six types is Doer, Thinker, Creator, Helper, Persuader, and Organizer. The following personality traits are often associated with Holland's personality types. Read them and place a check mark (✓) next to the descriptors that best fit you.

Realistic (Doer)
____ Practical
____ Frank
____ Reserved
____ Conservative
____ Active

Social (Helper)
____ Persuasive
____ Insightful
____ Extroverted
____ Helpful
____ Enthusiastic

Investigative (Thinker)
____ Achieving
____ Independent
____ Curious
____ Reserved
____ Planful

Enterprising (Persuader)
____ Dominant
____ Adventurous
____ Persuasive
____ Energetic
____ Sociable

Artistic (Creator)
____ Imaginative
____ Sensitive
____ Open
____ Creative
____ Expressive

Conventional (Organizer)
____ Responsible
____ Conforming
____ Orderly
____ Cautious
____ Good at detail

Clearly, most people are a combination of these six types but feel at home with two or three in particular. Add up your check marks (✓) for each type above and then write the names of the three personality types in which most of your check marks appeared:

1. _____   2. _____   3. _____

Identifying My Interests

An interest is a preference for certain types of activities. Interests hold one's attention or arouse one's curiosity. Generally, interests are learned—from your parents, from school subjects and activities, from friends, and from your life experiences. For example, when you engage in various activities, you react with specific feelings or attitudes. You like or dislike the activities, you feel challenged or bored, and you feel competent or clumsy. These personal reactions plus the feedback you receive on your performance (e.g., "You're really good at that") help to shape and focus your interests. You develop many interests during childhood and adolescence, and you continue to acquire interests throughout your life.

Interests can change. As you experience life and meet more people, you become interested in new things and discard some of your old interests. You also develop more complex thinking and understanding and seek new interests to improve yourself or to make life more exciting.

During the last two decades, interests have become the most important factor in measures of occupational selection. Most of us would like to work at something we enjoy. Career interest inventories have been developed to help identify interests and relate them to occupations. By measuring the interests of successful and satisfied people in an occupation, researchers have developed scales that compare the interests of these individuals to the interests of people who are uncertain about what they want to do. Thus, by comparing your interests to those of people who already are successful in specific occupations, you can identify occupations that you may wish to explore. This is the way the interests you have developed over the years can influence the occupational paths you choose. John Holland has developed interest inventories based on his theory of personality. The following interest inventory is reproduced from a version of Holland's Interest Inventory found on O*NET (www.onetcenter.org), a Web site sponsored by the U.S. Department of Labor. This exercise can help you identify your interests and continue your progress in the career decision-making process.

EXERCISE 2.2   Assessing My Interests

This activity describes various work activities that some people perform in their jobs. Read each description and place a check mark (✓) on the line next to those activities that you would *like* to do. Base your choices on whether you would *like* the activity, *not whether you have the education, training, or skill to perform the activity.*

Work Activities:

_____ **1.** Build kitchen cabinets
_____ **2.** Design landscape areas for yards and parks
_____ **3.** Work on automobiles
_____ **4.** Solve mechanical problems
_____ **5.** Design computer hardware
_____ **6.** Study the physical sciences
_____ **7.** Work with animals
_____ **8.** Operate machines on a production line

Total ✓s in Items 1–8 _____

_____ **9.** Study space travel
_____ **10.** Make a map of the bottom of the ocean
_____ **11.** Develop a new medicine
_____ **12.** Study ways to reduce pollution

____ **13.** Diagnose and treat sick animals

____ **14.** Study the personalities of world leaders

____ **15.** Conduct biological research

____ **16.** Study the governments of different countries

Total ✓s in Items 9–16 _____

____ **17.** Perform in a movie or television show

____ **18.** Act in a play

____ **19.** Announce a radio show

____ **20.** Write scripts for or edit movies, plays, or books

____ **21.** Write reviews of books or plays

____ **22.** Conduct or play in a symphony orchestra

____ **23.** Create dance routines for a show

____ **24.** Draw or paint pictures

Total ✓s in Items 17–24 _____

____ **25.** Perform nursing duties in a hospital

____ **26.** Help people with personal or emotional problems

____ **27.** Work with mentally disabled children or adults

____ **28.** Teach an elementary school class

____ **29.** Help people who have problems with drugs or alcohol

____ **30.** Organize activities at a recreational facility

____ **31.** Provide physical therapy to people recovering from an injury

____ **32.** Teach a high school class

Total ✓s in Items 25–32 _____

____ **33.** Operate a company or business

____ **34.** Sell computer equipment in a store

____ **35.** Market a new line of clothing

____ **36.** Negotiate business contracts

____ **37.** Represent a client in a lawsuit

____ **38.** Start your own business

____ **39.** Develop an accounting system for a business

____ **40.** Design Web sites

Total ✓s in Items 33–40 _____

____ **41.** Use a word processor to edit and format documents

____ **42.** Handle customers' bank transactions

____ **43.** Enter information into a database

____ **44.** Calculate the wages of employees

____ **45.** Assist senior-level accountants in performing bookkeeping tasks

____ **46.** Keep records of financial transactions for a business

____ **47.** Develop an office filing system

____ **48.** Transfer funds between banks using a computer

Total ✓s in Items 41–48 _____

In the following box, record the number of activities you checked (✓) "like" in each of the six numbered groups.

Items 1–8 _____ (Realistic)	Items 25–32 _____ (Social)
Items 9–16 _____ (Investigative)	Items 33–40 _____ (Enterprising)
Items 17–24 _____ (Artistic)	Items 41–48 _____ (Conventional)

Then read the descriptions of the Holland Occupational Interest Areas in Table 2.1. Circle the three groups in which you have the highest number of check marks (✓). Considering your results from above and the descriptions in Table 2.1, select the three Holland types that describe you best. Record them below: _____, _____, and _____

Table 2.1 Holland's Six Occupational Interest Areas

Realistic:

People with Realistic interests like work activities that include practical, hands-on problems and solutions. They enjoy dealing with plants, animals, and real-world materials, like wood, tools, and machinery. They enjoy outside work. Often people with Realistic interests do not like occupations that mainly involve doing paperwork or working closely with others.

Investigative:

People with Investigative interests like work activities that have to do with ideas and thinking more than with physical activity. They like to search for facts and figure out problems mentally rather than to persuade or lead people.

Artistic:

People with Artistic interests like work activities that deal with the artistic side of things, such as forms, designs, and patterns. They like self-expression in their work. They prefer settings where work can be done without following a clear set of rules.

Social:

People with Social interests like work activities that assist others and promote learning and personal development. They prefer to communicate rather than work with objects, machines, or data. They like to teach, to give advice, to help, or otherwise be of service to people.

Enterprising:

People with Enterprising interests like work activities that have to do with starting up and carrying out projects, especially business ventures. They like persuading and leading people and making decisions. They like taking risks for profit. These people prefer action rather than thought.

Conventional:

People with Conventional interests like work activities that follow set procedures and routines. They prefer working with data and detail more than with ideas. They prefer work in which there are precise standards rather than work in which you have to judge things by yourself. These people like working where the lines of authority are clear.

Identifying My Values

Values are those beliefs that are important to us and guide our choices and behavior. Your current values reflect the enculturation process that you have experienced thus far. As you have matured, you've modeled yourself after family members or other significant people in your life. Your family and significant others have reinforced the attitudes and behaviors that they hope will guide your life and influence your decisions. Honesty, independence, individualism, and personal responsibility are examples of values that may play important roles in your life and that you have learned from others. Values are central to the personal and career goals that we set for ourselves.

Work values are important to you in your work role. The U.S. Department of Labor recognizes the importance of work values and describes six main work values in its discussion of occupations found at the department's Web site (www.doleta.gov). A second list of work values is proposed by Ludden, Sharkin, and Farr (2001) in *Guide for Occupational Exploration*. You have a greater chance of being satisfied with your eventual academic and career choices if you consider which work values are most important to you. To identify which aspects of work are important to you, read the definitions of the major work values in Exercise 2.3, which are drawn from the sources cited above.

EXERCISE 2.3   Assessing My Work Values

Circle the number that best represents the importance of each work value to you:

Achievement: You can see the results of your efforts and feel you are accomplishing something.

| Less Important | 1 | 2 | 3 | 4 | 5 | 6 | More Important |

Autonomy: You plan your work with little supervision.

| Less Important | 1 | 2 | 3 | 4 | 5 | 6 | More Important |

Creativity: You like to create or design new things or present new ideas.

| Less Important | 1 | 2 | 3 | 4 | 5 | 6 | More Important |

Economic Returns: You desire work that pays well.

| Less Important | 1 | 2 | 3 | 4 | 5 | 6 | More Important |

Independence: You do things on your own initiative and may even work alone.

| Less Important | 1 | 2 | 3 | 4 | 5 | 6 | More Important |

Intellectual Stimulation: You like work that provides for ongoing learning.

| Less Important | 1 | 2 | 3 | 4 | 5 | 6 | More Important |

Recognition: You receive recognition for what you do.

| Less Important | 1 | 2 | 3 | 4 | 5 | 6 | More Important |

Relationships: You have colleagues at work who are friendly.

| Less Important | 1 | 2 | 3 | 4 | 5 | 6 | More Important |

Responsibility: You like to make decisions on your own.

| Less Important | 1 | 2 | 3 | 4 | 5 | 6 | More Important |

Service: You desire work where you can help other people.

| Less Important | 1 | 2 | 3 | 4 | 5 | 6 | More Important |

Social Status: You enjoy being looked up to by others.

| Less Important | 1 | 2 | 3 | 4 | 5 | 6 | More Important |

Supervision: You have supervisors who train you well and treat you fairly.

| Less Important | 1 | 2 | 3 | 4 | 5 | 6 | More Important |

Security: You like work that provides job security and good working conditions.

| Less Important | 1 | 2 | 3 | 4 | 5 | 6 | More Important |

Variety: You like to do different kinds of tasks at work.

| Less Important | 1 | 2 | 3 | 4 | 5 | 6 | More Important |

Table 2.2 Holland's Occupational Interests and Work Values	
Holland's Occupational Interest Area	**Work Values**
Realistic	Economic Returns Autonomy Achievement
Investigative	Responsibility Variety Achievement Intellectual Stimulation
Artistic	Creativity Autonomy Intellectual Stimulation
Social	Service Recognition Relationships Social Status
Enterprising	Recognition Economic Returns Relationships Variety
Conventional	Job Security Supervision Economic Returns

List the three work values that you rated the highest:

_____, _____, and _____. Are other work values also important to you? If so, add them to your list.

_____

Work values can be loosely matched to Holland's Occupational Interest Areas. In the right column of Table 2.2, circle the values you listed above. Then describe how and if your work values are compatible with the occupational interests you identified earlier.

_____
_____
_____
_____

Identifying My Skills

The skills you now possess and the ones you are willing to spend the effort to acquire will help determine the academic and career paths you choose. There is sometimes confusion about the difference between abilities and skills. Abilities are defined as our natural aptitudes or proficiencies. Skills can be acquired and are capacities that facilitate learning or the more rapid acquisition of knowledge.

Two- and four-year college degrees help you refine your basic skills and develop many others through course work and out-of-class activities. The U.S. Department of Labor has highlighted six sets of skills that are used in various work environments: Basic Skills, Complex Problem Solving Skills, Resource Management Skills, Social Skills, Systems Skills, and Technical Skills (www.careeronestop.org). The U.S. Department of Labor emphasizes that *all occupational areas require Basic Skills*. Knowing which skills are necessary to succeed in certain academic and occupational areas and the degree to which you possess them is an important consideration as you weigh your alternatives.

EXERCISE 2.4 My Skill Profile

The skills identified by the U.S. Department of Labor plus their definitions are listed below. Each skill set has been divided into sub-skills to allow you to develop a comprehensive profile of your skills. Place a check mark (✓) in front of the sub-skills in which you feel competent.

Basic Skills

Developed capacities that facilitate learning or the more rapid acquisition of knowledge:

_____ *Active Learning:* Understanding the implications of new information for both current and future problem solving and decision making.

_____ *Active Listening:* Giving full attention to what other people are saying, taking time to understand the points being made, asking questions as appropriate, and not interrupting at inappropriate times.

_____ *Critical Thinking:* Using logic and reasoning to identify the strengths and weaknesses of alternative solutions, conclusions, or approaches to problems.

_____ *Learning Strategies:* Selecting and using training/instructional methods and procedures appropriate for the situation when learning or teaching new things.

_____ *Mathematics:* Using mathematics to solve problems.

_____ *Monitoring:* Monitoring/assessing performance of yourself, other individuals, or organizations to make improvements or take corrective action.

✓ *Reading Comprehension:* Understanding written sentences and paragraphs in work-related documents.

_____ *Science:* Using scientific rules and methods to solve problems.

✓ *Speaking:* Talking to others to convey information effectively.

_____ *Writing:* Communicating effectively in writing as appropriate for the needs of the audience.

Complex Problem-Solving Skills

Developed capacities used to solve novel, ill-defined problems in complex, real-world settings:

_____ *Complex Problem Solving:* Identifying complex problems and reviewing related information to develop and evaluate options and implement solutions.

Resource Management Skills

Developed capacities used to allocate resources efficiently:

_____ *Management of Financial Resources:* Determining how money will be spent to get the work done, and accounting for these expenditures.

_____ *Management of Material Resources:* Obtaining and seeing to the appropriate use of equipment, facilities, and materials needed to do certain work.

_____ *Management of Personnel Resources:* Motivating, developing, and directing people as they work, identifying the best person for the job.

_____ *Time Management:* Managing one's own time and the time of others.

Social Skills

Developed capacities used to work with people to achieve goals:

✓ *Coordination:* Adjusting actions in relation to others' actions.

_____ *Instructing:* Teaching others how to do something.

✓ *Negotiation:* Bringing others together and trying to reconcile differences.

✓ *Persuasion:* Persuading others to change their minds or behavior.

✓ *Service Orientation:* Actively looking for ways to help people.

✓ *Social Perceptiveness:* Being aware of others' reactions and understanding why they react as they do.

Systems Skills

Developed capacities used to understand, monitor, and improve socio-technical systems:

_____ *Judgment and Decision Making:* Considering the relative costs and benefits of potential actions to choose the most appropriate one.

_____ *Systems Analysis:* Determining how a system should work and how changes in conditions, operations, and the environment will affect outcomes.

_____ *Systems Evaluation:* Identifying measures or indicators of system performance and the actions needed to improve or correct performance, relative to the goals of the system.

Technical Skills

Developed capacities used to design, set up, operate, and correct malfunctions involving application of machines or technological systems:

✓ *Equipment Maintenance:* Performing routine maintenance on equipment and determining when and what kind of maintenance is needed.

✓ *Equipment Selection:* Determining the kind of tools and equipment needed to do a job.

✓ *Installation:* Installing equipment, machines, wiring, or programs to meet specifications.

_____ *Operations Analysis:* Analyzing needs and product requirements to create a design.

_____ *Programming:* Writing computer programs for various purposes.

_____ *Quality Control Analysis:* Conducting tests and inspections of products, services, or processes to evaluate quality or performance.

List four or five skills that you believe are your strongest:

_____

_____

_____

List skills that others (e.g., your family and friends) have identified as your strengths. Add these to your list.

_____

_____

_____

List the skills that you still want to acquire and how you might acquire them:

_____

_____

_____

Some skills are associated with specific occupational interest areas more than others. Table 2.3 presents the Holland Occupational Interest Areas with which you are familiar and the skills that are associated with each Occupational Area. Note that Basic Skills are required in all occupations. In the right column of Table 2.3, circle the skills you identified above. Then answer the following question:

Which Occupational Areas best reflect the skills you now possess or plan to acquire? How do these areas compare with the ones you identified in assessing your interests and values?

_____

_____

_____

Table 2.3 Occupational Interest Areas and Associated Skills

Occupational Interest Area	Associated Skills
Realistic	Basic Skills (e.g., Reading, Science) Systems Evaluation Skills Social Skills (e.g., Instructing) Technical Skills (e.g. equipment selection and equipment maintenance)
Investigative	Basic Skills Quality Control Analysis System Skills (e.g., Judgment and Decision Making) and, in some cases, Systems Analysis Programming Equipment Selection Complex Problem Solving
Artistic	Basic Skills Technical Skills (e.g., equipment selection and maintenance) Monitoring Coordination Social Perceptiveness
Social	Basic Skills Service Orientation Instructing Negotiating Social Perceptiveness
Enterprising	Basic Skills Management of Financial Resources Management of Personnel Resources Negotiating, Persuasion, and Service Orientation (in some cases)
Conventional	Basic Skills Systems Analysis Systems Evaluation Coordination (in some cases) Judgment and Decision Making

Summary Profile #1: My Personal Characteristics

So far, you have identified and assessed important personal characteristics that will influence your career and academic choices. Knowing more about your personality characteristics, interests, values, and skills can lead to more informed occupational decisions. Summarize how you would assess yourself at this point:

List three personality types that best describe you. (Review Exercise 2.1 on page 11):

_____, _____, and _____

List your three highest occupational interests (Exercise 2.2 on page 12):

_____, _____, and _____

List your most important work values (Exercise 2.3 on page 15):

_____, _____, and _____

List the skills you see as your strongest (Exercise 2.4 on page 17):

_____, _____, and _____

Write two or three statements in which you summarize how your personality type, interests, work values, and skills may have influenced your major and occupational decisions to this point.

Share your statements with someone who knows you well and ask him or her to give you feedback on your summary.

HOW DOES MY ENVIRONMENT INFLUENCE MY CAREER CHOICES

Career theorist John Krumboltz suggests that environmental factors influence career decision making. Since the early 1950s, sociologists have explored how career decisions are affected by social environment. Family and socioeconomic status, general economic conditions, society's stereotypes about specific occupations, and its attitudes about multicultural populations all influence career development.

Socioeconomic Status (SES)

Your social and economic background is related to your family's resources. You inherit from your parents certain financial and other resources that, to some extent, influence your career choices. Your family's financial status determines things such as where you live and what schools you attend. In turn, these can affect your values, occupational expectations, opportunities, and gender-role expectations. Because social status often is passed down from generation to generation, you may have benefited by being exposed to many opportunities or, on the other hand, you may not yet have had the opportunity to recognize all the career options open to you.

Even though your SES may have affected your career ideas so far, many career-related decisions lie ahead. High aspirations and motivation to achieve will help you reach your goals. In Exercise 2.5, indicate how your socioeconomic status has affected your career options and thinking.

EXERCISE 2.5 Exploring Socioeconomic Status

Think about your family. How would you describe your socioeconomic level (lower, middle, upper)?

How has your SES influenced which schools you have attended?

How has your family influenced your ideas about your career?

Family Influences

Additional aspects of your family background can be influential in career decision making. In studies of college students' career development, researchers have found that parents were the most influential career role models for students. Mothers seemed to exert the greatest influence during their children's high school years, and fathers seemed more influential in their college-aged children's decisions. Exercise 2.6 is designed to help you think about ways your family has influenced your career development.

EXERCISE 2.6 A Career Genogram

A genogram is a graphic representation of your biological and stepgrandparents, parents, aunts, uncles, and siblings. Complete the genogram to help you identify models who may have influenced your occupational perceptions, as well as the perceptions you have of yourself as a worker. You may need to talk with your parents or other relatives to complete this activity.

GENOGRAM

Put in initials of family members in the parentheses below each relative (use stepparents/siblings when applicable), and write their occupations on the lines below, if known.

MATERNAL

Grandmother (JK) Bycologist		Grandfather (EK) Bycologist				Grandmother (PG)		Grandfather (JG) musician

PATERNAL

Aunt (LK) Lonneleys	Uncle (DK) Teacher	Aunt ( )	MOTHER (DS)	Uncle ( )	Uncle ( )	Aunt ( )	Uncle ( )	FATHER (EG) machinist	Aunt ( )	Uncle (JG) electrician

Cousin ( )	Cousin ( )	Cousin (BG)	Cousin ( )	Cousin ( )	Cousin ( )	Cousin ( )	Cousin (MG) HighSchool	Cousin (BG) Navy

Sibling (VG) Vettech	Sibling (WS) rancher	Sibling ( )

After you have completed your Career Genogram, answer the following questions:

1. Do any occupations show up repeatedly? If so, which ones?

   _____

2. Do any general career fields show up repeatedly (e.g., business, medicine)? If so, which ones?

   _____

3. What levels of socioeconomic status are reflected in your genogram (e.g., blue collar, white collar, professional)?

   _____

4. What were the attitudes toward work in your family (e.g., important, unimportant, enjoyable, not enjoyable)?

   _____

   _____

5. What were the work values in your family (e.g., independence, security, high salaries)?

   _____

   _____

   _____

6. What behaviors and attitudes were reinforced as they related to males and females?

   _____

   _____

7. Did both of your parents work outside the home? _____ Yes _____ No
   If they both worked, how did that influence you? If only one worked, how did that influence you?

   _____

   _____

   _____

8. How did your parents and grandparents handle the multiple roles of worker, spouse, parent, and child?

   _____

   _____

   _____

9. What life role do you think your parents believe is most important for you (e.g., worker, spouse, parent, child, citizen)? Briefly explain your answer.

   _____

   _____

   _____

10. Do any family members have unfulfilled dreams they are trying to live vicariously through you? If so, who and how?

    _____

    _____

    _____

    _____

    _____

11. As you think about your answers to these questions, what influence do you think your family has had on your career development and decision making?

    _____

    _____

_____

_____

_____

_____

The Impact of Gender

Whether you are female or male has influenced some of the choices you have made, as well as some of the choices your parents made for you. For instance, gender might have influenced the toys you were given, whether you were encouraged to take risks, your high school curriculum, and, in some cases, your choice of academic major. Often gender-related messages are subtle and their influence is difficult to discern. For example, if three generations of women in your family have been homemakers and you are a woman considering an engineering career, your beliefs and attitudes about women who work outside the home may produce conflict in your career choice. Consider the "what ifs" by completing Exercise 2.7.

EXERCISE 2.7   What If?

Take a few minutes to write a paragraph entitled "How My Life Would Be Different If I Had Been Born of the Opposite Sex (Female or Male)." (Write from the perspective of the opposite sex.) Include comments about your parents' and other relatives' expectations, high school courses and activities, teachers, and any other influences, such as the media.

_____

_____

_____

_____

_____

_____

_____

_____

_____

_____

_____

_____

What themes are apparent in the paragraph you wrote?

_____

_____

_____

_____

Do you think your gender has influenced your career or major choices? How?

_____

_____

_____

Other Environmental Factors

We have discussed only a few of the environmental factors (socioeconomic status [SES], family background, occupational stereotyping) that can influence your career development. Other factors can be influential, too. For example, some researchers suggest that middle-class parents tend to value self-direction in their children, whereas parents with lower SES tend to value conformity. Self-direction and conformity are important characteristics and may be reflected in the choices we make as adults. Also, those who study childrearing practices suggest that boys are more apt than girls to be encouraged to take risks and assert themselves. Do these implications lead to differences in career choices? As researchers continue to try to answer these questions, you can challenge your own thinking and examine your personal beliefs. Don't underestimate yourself.

Answer the questions in Summary Profile #2 to summarize how your environment has influenced your ideas about a career choice.

Summary Profile #2 Environmental Influences on My Career Development and Choices

Socioeconomic Status

Briefly summarize how your socioeconomic status may have influenced your career decision making.

_____

_____

_____

_____

Family Background

Briefly summarize how your family's occupational choices, work attitudes, and work values may have influenced your career decision making:

_____

_____

_____

_____

Impact of Gender

Briefly summarize how being born male or female in our society may have influenced your career decision making.

_____

_____

_____

PULLING IT ALL TOGETHER

This chapter helped you examine the personal characteristics that make you a unique individual. You identified and reflected upon your personality traits, interests, work values, and skills to give you insights about who you are, what you are good at, and what is important to you. In addition, you examined how environmental influences such as socioeconomic status, gender, and family background may have influenced your career development. Summary Profiles #1 and #2 helped you pull together information about all these factors. Use Exercise 2.8 to review what you have learned about yourself. In Chapter Three you will have the opportunity to integrate what you have learned about yourself with occupational information.

EXERCISE 2.8   Reviewing My Options

Take a few minutes to review what you have learned about yourself in Chapter Two that might influence the occupations and majors that you will explore in the next two chapters.

_____

_____

_____

_____

_____

_____

CASE STUDIES

Exploring

JED

When Jed reflected on how he answered the questions in Chapter Two, he was surprised at how much he really knew about his interests and skills. Two of the areas of the self-assessment activities that offered new insights were in identifying his work values and in evaluating the influence his family has on the occupational choices he is considering. Although he seriously had considered joining the family business, his Summary Profiles revealed a strong interest in the career areas of Social and Realistic.

A career in teaching, coaching, or fitness always had interested him, but he was afraid the economic rewards would not be great enough to satisfy him. His work values activity reflected differently since he had selected autonomy, relationships, and variety as his three most important work values. Jed has decided he needs more information about other occupational fields that might match his interests and values.

MARIA

Working with a computer programmer for 2 hours a day, Maria has become increasingly interested in this type of work. She likes the problem solving opportunities involved as well as the logic and detail in this work. Maria has always wanted to attend college but wasn't sure if she could be successful. She knows, however, that this and any other work she may want to do in the future will require more education. The career course she has been taking at her local community college has helped her experience a college environment and opened her eyes to many different career possibilities, both in the computer field and in others. She was not surprised that her Summary Profile reflected her interests and skills in the Conventional and Enterprising types. Also reflected were her work values (autonomy, job security, and economic returns). After discussing her profile and situation with her course instructor, he reinforced her belief that she could be successful in college and encouraged her to talk to faculty in computer science and related majors. ■

Summary Checklist

WHAT I HAVE LEARNED

_____ I realize that knowing my personality traits and limitations is critical in the career-planning process.

_____ I now understand the interaction between personality, interests, skills, and values in the career-planning process.

_____ I have a better understanding of how my family background and other environmental factors have influenced my knowledge and attitudes about work.

HOW I CAN USE IT

By learning about my personal characteristics and reflecting upon how environmental factors have influenced my own career development, I am better prepared to think about exploring more realistic occupational possibilities.

CHAPTER 3

How Do I Search for Occupational Information?

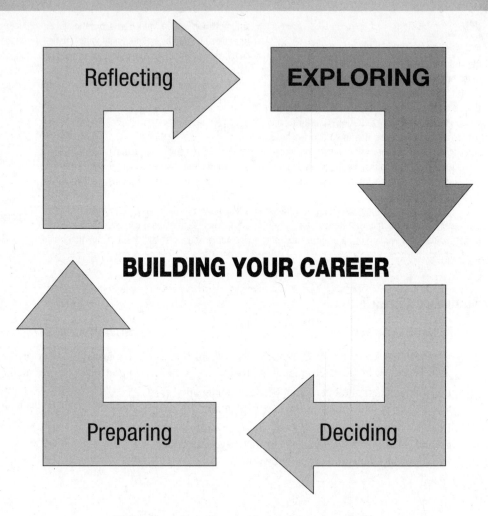

"'Tis true; there's magic in the web of it."

SHAKESPEARE, *OTHELLO*

How many occupations do I really know anything about? How can I find accurate and reliable occupational information so I can make important career decisions? This chapter will help you answer those questions. Accurate and current occupational information can help you narrow the number of career areas you are considering, correct stereotypes about specific occupations, and generate opportunities you may not have considered. In this chapter you will:

- locate sources of accurate and timely occupational information,
- learn how to conduct informational interviews, and
- combine what you have learned about your personality, skills, and values with the occupational information you are gathering.

STARTING MY SEARCH

Where do you begin these challenging tasks? What occupations do you want to learn more about?

EXERCISE 3.1   **What Occupations Interest Me?**

Write down the first three occupations that come to mind when you ask yourself what occupations interest you:

1. _____

2. _____

3. _____

Was it easy or difficult to think of three? Some people have difficulty selecting occupations to explore because they know so little about the work tasks involved, the training required, salary ranges, and many other factors. To help you add to your list, Table 3.1 provides examples of a few occupations that are compatible with each Holland type. (You were introduced to John Holland in Chapter Two when you used his career theory to identify your interests, values, and skills and compared them with Holland's types). Uing the same descriptors as his personality types

Table 3.1 Personality and Career Choices

Realistic	Social
Mechanical engineer	Fitness trainer
Horticulturalist	Nurse
Military officer	Historian
Robotic technologist	Physical therapist
Financial analyst	Economist
Law enforcer	Criminalist
Architectural technologist	Social science teacher
Zookeeper	Counselor
Computer engineer	Market research analyst
Medical technologist	Travel agent

Investigative	Enterprising
Website developer	Financial planner
Chemist	Human resources officer
Pharmacist	Lawyer
Computer engineer	Personnel manager
Mathematician	Radio/TV announcer
Veterinarian	Recreation director
Electrical engineer	Chief executive
Microbiologist	Computer systems analyst
Respiratory therapist	Hotel manager
Physician	Sports director

Artistic	Conventional
Artist	Accountant
Interior decorator	Finance expert
Editor	Curator
Musician	Advertising manager
Preschool administrator	Tax consultant
Animator	Electrical drafter
Art teacher	Convention planner
Landscape architect	Cartographer
Illustrator	Bank teller

(Realistic, Investigative, Social, Enterprising, Artistic, and Conventional), Holland theorizes that occupations can be categorized into six work environments and that most people are happiest when their personality is congruent with their work environment. For example, business work environments often attract individuals with Enterprising and Conventional personalities because of the work tasks demanded in those specific work environments. Table 3.1 provides a few examples of occupations in each of Holland's six work environments to get you started. (Keep in mind that each occupation has a three-type code, with the first type being the predominant one.)

EXERCISE 3.2   **Developing a List of Occupations to Search**

Write additional occupations that you want to add to your list of possible careers:

1. _____
2. _____
3. _____
4. _____

You will be using these later in Exercise 3.3.

SOURCES OF OCCUPATIONAL INFORMATION

What facts are needed to make occupational information helpful? Some of the information about specific occupations that you will want to gather includes:

- the nature of the work performed in that occupation,
- education and training requirements for entry and advancement,
- outlook for current and future employment options/possibilities,
- earnings and benefits,
- personal qualifications needed (skills and aptitudes),
- working conditions, and
- related occupations.

Occupational information is plentiful! Major sources include Internet Web sites, career guidance systems, direct or firsthand experience, and informational interviews. Different sources offer different types of information. If you collect information from someone who knows you, your interests, skills, and qualifications, you will receive specific and personal information delivered informally. Information from Internet sources may seem less personal but usually is very comprehensive. Direct or firsthand experience, however, gives you a feel for an occupation that reading alone just can't provide. Gathering information from a range of sources is the best way to determine the occupations that might interest you the most.

The Internet

By far, the Internet has more and more varied information than any other source. Access to occupational and other career-related information, such as interest inventories and skill assessments, are available to you on many Internet sites. Your college or university may provide access to Internet services in your dorm, career services office, or libraries. No single Web site contains all the information you need, but some are more comprehensive than others. Exercise 3.3 will introduce you to O*NET, a U.S. government Web site. This well-known resource will help you explore specific occupations in depth.

O*NET

The *Occupational Information Network* (O*NET, www.onetcenter.org), developed by the U.S. Department of Labor, is the nation's primary resource center for occupational information, includes a database that contains information on hundreds of occupations, and is free to use. Another advantage is that the Department of Labor continually updates the information by surveying a broad range of workers from each occupation. The information on O*NET forms the core of

O*NET OnLine, an interactive application for searching occupations. For Exercise 3.3, you need to access O*NET online (online.onetcenter.org).

EXERCISE 3.3   **Using O*NET Online to Explore Occupations**

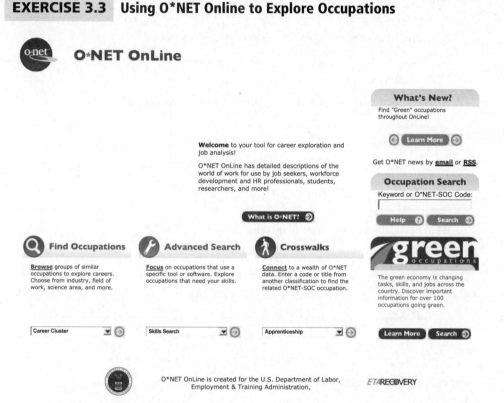

Source: O*NET OnLine was created for the U.S. Department of Labor, Employment & Training Administration by the National Center for O*NET Development.

- Go to online.onetcenter.org.
- Click on "Find Occupations".
- Go to "Keyword" or "O*NET-SOC" in the upper left corner of the page.
- Key in the occupation you wish to explore in the box and click "Go".
- A list of matching or relevant occupations will appear. Click directly on the title/name of the occupation you want to explore.
- A "Summary Report" for that occupation will appear on the screen and describe the major tasks of the occupation, tools and technology used, knowledge needed, skills needed, abilities required, work activities related to the occupation, interests, work styles, work values, related occupations, and wages.
- Use Occupational Search Worksheets #1 and #2 on pages 29–30 to gather information about at least two of the occupations you are exploring.

Occupational Search Worksheet #1

1. Name of occupation:

   _____

2. What are the major tasks associated with this occupation?

   _____

   _____

   _____

3. What are the primary knowledge, skills, and abilities required?

   _____

   _____

   _____

4. What three or four work activities are related to this occupation?

_____

_____

_____

5. What are the interests of those in this occupation?

_____

_____

6. What are the work values of those interested in this occupation?

_____

_____

7. What are the typical wages paid for this occupation?

_____

_____

8. What occupations are related to this one?

_____

_____

9. What are the costs and benefits of this occupation?

_____

_____

_____

Occupational Search Worksheet #2

1. Name of occupation:

_____

2. What are the major tasks associated with this occupation?

_____

_____

_____

3. What are the primary knowledge, skills, and abilities required?

_____

_____

_____

4. What three or four work activities are related to this occupation?

_____

_____

_____

5. What are the interests of those in this occupation?

_____

_____

6. What are the work values of those interested in this occupation?

_____

_____

7. What are the typical wages paid for this occupation?

_____

_____

8. What occupations are related to this one?

_____

_____

9. What are the costs and benefits of this occupation?

_____

_____

_____

Repeat the same search process for any of the occupations that you identified in Exercises 3.1 and 3.2 in this chapter. Share the occupational information you have gathered with your classmates. If you have any questions about the searches or the search process, consult your instructor. Of all the occupations you searched as a part of this exercise, which interested you the most? Why?

_____

_____

_____

_____

Other Internet Resources

Many other Internet resources are available, and several are highlighted in this section. Since Internet site addresses change so frequently, U.S. Department of Labor or government Web sites are emphasized here. Government sites are comprehensive and fairly stable, and if an address changes, you usually are directed to a new site.

OCCUPATIONAL OUTLOOK HANDBOOK The *Occupational Outlook Handbook* (www.bls. gov/oco) is an excellent source of accurate and timely information. For hundreds of occupations, it describes:

- the training and education needed,
- earnings,
- expected job prospects,
- what workers do on the job, and
- working conditions.

The *Handbook* categorizes occupations using ten occupational groups. In addition, the *Handbook* links you to job search tips and information about the job market in each state. If you know where you want to live when you graduate, consider reviewing employment projections in that state. You will be using this Web site in Chapter Six to explore some of these factors.

CAREERONESTOP This Web site (www.careeronestop.org) has tools to help you and other students, career professionals, job seekers, and businesses explore information about occupations. You can also use CareerOneStop to access self-assessments or tools to explore your skills, interests, and values much like those you completed in Chapter Two. Career videos describing skills and interests needed in over 500 occupations will help you consider a wide range of occupations. You may want to bookmark this site for future reference because it includes links to several other U.S. Department of Labor Web sites, including the following:

- *State Job Banks* allows you to search over a million job openings listed with state employment agencies.
- *America's Career InfoNet* provides data on employment growth and wages by occupation; the knowledge, skills, and abilities required by an occupation; and links to employers.
- *America's Service Locator* includes a comprehensive database of career centers and information on unemployment benefits, job training, youth programs, seminars, educational opportunities, and disabled or older worker programs.

USAJOBS USAJOBS (www.usajobs.gov) is the official job site of the U.S. federal government. You will find information about all federal jobs plus jobs for students at this Web site. This site includes a Veteran's Employment Resource Center with tools and resources for all U.S. veterans.

Career Guidance Systems

Career guidance–based approaches are another source of information and include both occupational information and some type of career-planning system to help you gather and organize information about yourself (self-assessments of your interests, values, and skills), occupations of interest, and career planning. Some provide information about academic majors, financial aid, military employment opportunities, and job seeking skills such as résumé writing and job search strategies. One of the primary advantages of career guidance systems is that they can help you organize some of the data that you are collecting. They also store your data, if you choose, so you can come back to your career plan or portfolio as often as you like to try out different scenarios to discover what might "fit" the best. Most systems wisely encourage you to seek the services of an on-site professional to help you better understand your printouts and the process you are experiencing. You usually can find one or more of these career guidance systems in the career services or advising center at your college or university.

Three of the more popular systems are described briefly in the following subsections, and the URL for each is included so you can access them at your college's career service or advising center if they are available.

DISCOVER   *DISCOVER* (www.act.org/discover/overview/index.html) includes research-based assessments of interests, abilities, and job values and uses a World-of-Work Map that organizes occupations into six clusters that reflect John Holland's career theory (refer to Chapter Two). This system offers you the opportunity to explore databases of occupations, college majors, schools/training institutions, financial aid and military options. You can also develop your job-seeking skills (résumés, cover letters, job applications, and interviewing) using either an Internet version or one delivered via CD-ROMs.

FOCUS V.2   *FOCUS V.2* (www.focuscareer2.com) is both a career exploration and an education planning system designed for college students. If your university or college uses this system, you will be able to match your online assessment results to the major areas of study at your institution.

SIGI 3   *SIGI 3* (www.valparint.com), the System of Integrated Guidance and Information, is the third generation of a program originally developed in the 1980s by the Educational Testing Service (ETS). This career guidance system allows you to take self-assessments with a focus on values and then helps you integrate those assessments with current career information to develop a career plan.

Direct Experience

Direct or firsthand experience, another source of occupational information, allows you to match your skills against those required for a specific occupation. It can serve as a reality check for your decision making by providing an opportunity to see if the work really interests you. Volunteering during summers or weekends or interning in a preferred occupation allows you to determine if your work values are compatible with those in specific career areas. Also, working in a setting in which you can observe others in the same or similar occupations can provide insight into your own career decision making and confirm or challenge your career choices. Further, interning, co-oping, or part-time work may enhance your résumé or give you contacts and references once you graduate.

Informational Interviews

Interviewing workers already in an occupation is one of the more stimulating ways for you to collect information about occupations. Talking directly to individuals at their workplaces allows you to get a sense or feel of what it would be like for you to work in a similar setting. The primary advantage of informational interviews is the firsthand knowledge you gain about the occupation, the work environment, and work tasks or activities. The main disadvantage is that you hear only one perspective about the occupation in only one particular setting. Still an informational interview can help you confirm or question choices that you are considering. If, while still attending college, you can participate in an internship in a career that interests you, use an Informational Interview Worksheet (see Exercise 3.4) to conduct an interview of a worker at your site. Responses to those questions plus your own experience should give you insight into the true nature of the work in that occupational area. You will be conducting more interviews in Chapter Four (College Majors) and Chapter Eight (Job Interviews). Some suggestions for conducting productive interviews follow.

Conducting Informational Interviews

Be professional: Review the questions on the Informational Interview Worksheet (Exercise 3.4) to prepare; show genuine interest.

Be punctual: If you ask for a certain amount of time (e.g., 20 or 30 minutes), stick to it.

Dress appropriately: No shorts, T-shirts, or tank tops.

Use positive body language: Maintain eye contact, and sit forward in your chair.

Listen carefully: Take notes and ask clarifying questions.

Show appreciation: Thank your interviewee immediately after the interview and send a written thank-you note the next day (or sooner) after the interview (many employers prefer a written note over an e-mail message).

EXERCISE 3.4   Conducting an Informational Interview

Consult with your instructor or college adviser for help in arranging an interview with someone who works in one or two of the occupations you searched on the Internet. Use one of the following Informational Interview Worksheets. (Photocopy the questions if you need more than two forms.)

Informational Interview Worksheet #1

Name of occupation:

_____

1. What are your major work activities?

   _____

   _____

   _____

2. What knowledge and skills do you need for this work?

   _____

   _____

3. What is a typical day like in your work?

   _____

   _____

   _____

4. What are the working conditions on your job (e.g., hours, dress requirements, work environment, salary)?

   _____

   _____

5. What led you to choose this occupation?

   _____

   _____

6. How did you prepare for your job?

   _____

   _____

7. If you were hiring someone for your job, what qualifications would you want him or her to have?

   _____

   _____

   _____

8. What is the employment outlook for your job?

_____

_____

9. What other occupations are related to this one?

_____

_____

10. What advice would you give someone who is thinking about pursuing this occupation?

_____

_____

Reflection on What You Have Learned

1. What was the most important information you learned from the interview? Why?

_____

_____

_____

2. What did you learn that would prove useful in your occupational search?

_____

_____

_____

3. What are your current thoughts about the suitability of this occupation for you?

_____

_____

_____

Informational Interview Worksheet #2

Name of occupation:

1. What are your major work activities?

_____

_____

_____

2. What knowledge and skills do you need for this work?

_____

_____

_____

3. What is a typical day like in your work?

_____

_____

_____

4. What are the working conditions on your job (e.g., hours, dress requirements, work environment, salary)?

_____

_____

5. What led you to choose this occupation?

_____

_____

6. How did you prepare for your job?

_____

_____

7. If you were hiring someone for your job, what qualifications would you want him or her to have?

_____

_____

8. What is the employment outlook for your job?

_____

_____

9. What other occupations are related to this one?

_____

_____

10. What advice would you give someone who is thinking about pursuing this occupation?

_____

_____

Reflection on What I Have Learned

1. What was the most important information you learned from the interview? Why?

_____

_____

2. What did you learn that would prove useful in your occupational search?

_____

_____

3. What are your current thoughts about the suitability of this occupation for you?

_____

_____

In class, discuss the last three questions on the Informational Interview Worksheet. Did Exercise 3.4 help you narrow down your choices?

_____

_____

Narrowing Down My Choices

In Chapter Two, you examined your personal traits, interests, values, and skills. In this chapter you conducted occupational searches on the Internet and interviewed a worker or workers in your areas of interest. At this point, you should be ready to identify some tentative occupational choices. List the occupations that appeal most to you. You will be adding to your information about related college majors and other factors in the chapters that follow.

1. _____

2. _____

3. _____

CASE STUDIES

Exploring

JED

Jed spent several hours on the O*NET Web site. He was amazed and sometimes a little overwhelmed at the amount of information about each occupation. Once he slowed down and thought about what he was reading, he began to see the similarities among the occupations he was exploring. In many ways, teaching and coaching were very much alike. He also recognized, however, that teaching is a changing occupation. Teachers are using computers much more than he realized. He decided that if he pursues a teaching career, he better take a couple of computer-related courses so he can improve his skills. Jed interviewed a teacher and a fitness trainer. He is still undecided but thinks he could be happy in either of these career fields.

MARIA

Maria couldn't believe all of the detailed occupational information on O*NET. She spent several nights on the Internet exploring computer occupations. She was amazed at the variety of jobs in the computer field. She liked what she read about computer programmers and began to search other sources for more information. She was especially interested in finding out about the educational and training requirements for the different jobs in this area. ■

Summary Checklist

WHAT I HAVE LEARNED

____ I know where to locate occupational information.

____ I know what a source needs to include to make it helpful and reliable.

____ I know how to conduct an occupational search on the Internet and can use these skills when needed.

____ I have learned how to interview workers in the area of my interest and can use this strategy again if I need to modify my decision(s).

HOW I CAN USE IT

I now have solid occupational information upon which to base my career decisions. If I need to reconsider my choices in the future, I will know how to find the information resources that work best for me.

What Do I Need to Know About Educational Alternatives?

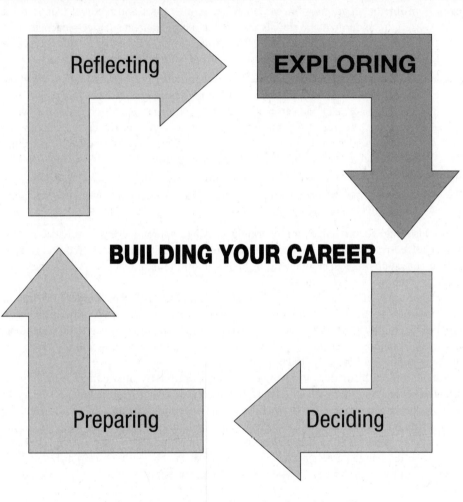

Reflecting

EXPLORING

BUILDING YOUR CAREER

Preparing

Deciding

"It is the mark of an educated mind to be able to entertain a thought without accepting it."

ARISTOTLE

CHOOSING AN EDUCATIONAL DIRECTION

As you formulate more definitive occupational plans, your choices about your education become an important consideration. Whether you are a first-year college student, a sophomore, or an older adult pondering a career change, selecting the appropriate type and level of education is a multifaceted decision. Your career aspirations often suggest or even dictate the type and level of educational preparation you need to enter the workforce. For example, if you wish to become a social worker aide, you will want to attend a two-year college that will give you direct occupational training for that work. If you wish to be a social worker, you will need a baccalaureate degree. If you wish to be a social agency administrator, you would do best to obtain a graduate degree (e.g., a master's in social work [MSW], a master's in counseling [MA], or a master's in public administration [MPA]).

The U.S. Department of Labor describes several educational programs that provide the knowledge and skills required at different levels of occupations:

Graduate   Occupations such as business manager or college professor often require graduate studies involving one or more years of schooling beyond the baccalaureate degree. Examples of graduate degrees are an MBA (master's in business administration), an MFA (master's of fine arts), or a Ph.D. (doctoral degree).

College   Some occupations—for example, museum curator and medical technologist—require undergraduate studies that lead to a baccalaureate degree—bachelor of arts (BA) or bachelor of science (BS). Most community colleges offer a two-year degree that can also fulfill the first two years of a baccalaureate degree.

Technical   Technical programs beyond the high school level prepare the student for specific occupations or teach skills needed for a particular type of work. Earning a technical degree usually takes from six months to two years and often leads to a two-year associate's degree (AA) or a certificate (e.g., an AA in engineering technology or a professional nanny certificate). This type of preparation is offered at technical schools, community colleges, and some four-year colleges and universities.

Vocational   High school level vocational programs fall into this category. These programs focus on specific occupations or skills. Examples include automotive technology and health technology.

You also may acquire education or training through apprenticeships, military service, or other specialized programs. A few occupations, such as cashier and clerk, require no formal training or education other than a general or high school diploma, but on-the-job experience is required for some jobs in the trades.

Some occupations require credentials such as licenses, certificates, degrees, or diplomas. To work in professional occupations (e.g., health, architecture, education), you probably will need to follow a highly structured educational program specifically designed to prepare students for state and/or national licensing or certification tests. Formal education and training are fast becoming prerequisites for jobs in today's work world.

Although the information in this chapter focuses primarily on a college education, it is important to become familiar with other educational options as well. Some students select a two-year college but later transfer to a four-year program. Other students enroll in a four-year college and discover that a two-year technical degree would be better suited to their interests, abilities, and career goals. Keep in mind that any decision you make now is not necessarily permanent. You may wish to change careers at any age, and a new career may require a different type of education or training. In Exercise 4.1 you will answer the question of what type of education you might need.

EXERCISE 4.1 What Type of Education Do I Need?

What education do you want to complete (e.g., four-year college degree, technical degree, graduate degree)?

_____

_____

_____

Do you need other information to confirm this choice? If so, where will you obtain it (e.g., college admissions office, college catalogues, professional organizations, academic advisors, college faculty)?

_____

_____

_____

How does this type of education fit with your future goals? For example, will you need a four-year degree in business to obtain a job in the field you are considering?

_____

_____

_____

Why Attend College?

People attend college for many reasons. Some consider it preparation for a job. Others value a college degree for the broad education it provides. They enjoy learning for learning's sake. Still others consider it a personal accomplishment. Our value system often determines the reasons we enroll in higher education. In Exercise 4.2 you will consider why you are in college.

EXERCISE 4.2   Why Am I in College?

Following are some academic, personal, and career reasons for attending college. Read them all and then check the five that are most important to you.

_____ To learn for the sake of learning

_____ To become proficient in reading and study skills

__✓__ To improve my ability to think and reason

_____ To broaden my intellectual interests

_____ To choose an area of study that will be interesting and challenging to me

_____ To enjoy a variety of cultural activities

__✓__ To learn how to become an effective leader

_____ To make my family proud of me

_____ To make lifelong friends

_____ To participate in the social opportunities on campus

__✓__ To take courses that lead directly to an occupational field

__✓__ To learn the skills necessary to find a good job when I graduate

_____ To prepare myself for a certain lifestyle

__✓__ To help me make more money in my work

_____ To prepare for graduate school

Are the five reasons you checked above mainly academic, personal, or career-related? What does this tell you?

_____

_____

How do these reasons affect your life as a student? How will they affect you after graduation?

_____

_____

Making Initial Decisions

Charlie decided in high school to become an engineer. His teachers encouraged him to use his math and science abilities in a career. Charlie's father and sister are professional engineers, so he had experience working in an engineering firm during the summers. Charlie declared an engineering major when he entered college. Although he is not sure what branch of engineering he wants to pursue, he is certain he has made the right choice.

Some students like Charlie enter college with specific career aspirations. They are aware of their abilities and interests and, through their research and experience, understand exactly what is expected in a particular work environment. These students have put careful thought into their decisions, often based on solid information and experiences. If you were as "decided" as Charlie, you might not be reading this book.

Though most students have several possible majors in mind, they may not be ready to make a choice.

> Carla had many interests when she entered college but was not ready to declare a major. She chose to be "undecided" and entered a special advising program for students who are unsure of their major. Carla's strengths are in language, art, and the social sciences. She can test her ideas before deciding on a major by taking a variety of courses in these areas. Her academic advisor is helping her sort through her options. Carla also has visited the college's career center, where she is gathering information about herself and possible majors and careers.

It is common for students to be undecided during the first year of college. At some point, though, they will need to spend time purposefully exploring possible careers. Some campuses have excellent resources to assist students with this exploration. Most colleges and universities have a career planning center that offers career counseling, testing, a career library, and computerized career information systems. Students who are not sure about their direction need to take responsibility for actively researching various occupational options. The skills they use in doing this will prove useful as they make decisions throughout their college years and beyond.

> Sam entered college and declared a business major. He was not certain that he wanted to be a businessman at the time, but he chose that area because he wanted a well-paying job after college. Sam was bored and did not do well in several of his core business classes. He did do well, however, in his English and social science courses. By the middle of his sophomore year, he knew he wanted to change his major. He worked with his academic advisor, who helped him to identify other majors more closely related to his interests and abilities.

While first-year college students are exploring their options, upper-level students sometimes find that their initial choice of major is not as satisfying as they originally thought and now want to change direction. They discover that they have no interest in or talent for their initial choices. They are in a different situation from that of first-year students, because now they have a record of coursework that may give them insight into their strengths and limitations. Other students, particularly at large universities, find they are closed out of certain majors because of highly selective admissions requirements.

Once Sam recognized his desire to change majors, he sought help. After carefully appraising his strengths and limitations, he selected a public relations major because it fulfilled his interest and talent in writing and his desire to work in a business setting. Unfortunately, some students do not follow Sam's path; they leave school before examining all of their alternatives.

> During high school Angie worked part-time answering phones at a hospital and became interested in preparing for a job in a health-related field. She sought an education that would be practical, give her hands-on experience, and prepare her to enter a specific occupation. She enrolled in a local community college program in emergency medical technology. When she completes her training, she will be certified as a paramedic. She now works in the hospital emergency room part-time while going to school. Angie is very excited about her future.

Technical education meets the needs of many students who want to learn specific skills. Earning an associate's degree is an excellent avenue for students who want practical preparation for a challenging and satisfying career.

The Undergraduate Curriculum

One of the biggest differences between a two- and four-year degree is the curriculum. A technical education focuses on acquiring the skills needed to perform certain tasks in a technical occupation. Some two-year associate degrees fulfill the requirements for the first two years of a baccalaureate degree. Four-year degrees, however, usually include a general introduction to many subjects with the intent of providing students with a broad base of knowledge in addition to a specialization or major.

Most baccalaureate degree programs have specific course requirements, including courses in the humanities, social sciences, and sciences. Some majors require students to take certain courses in a related area. For example, a student with an engineering major must take physics classes. Some colleges require students to take courses with an international or a multicultural focus.

Technical programs such as computer science often have basic course requirements that include writing and math components. These basic courses, rather than offering a general approach, focus on specific skills applicable to the pertinent technical area.

Many baccalaureate programs are highly structured and allow students limited opportunities to take elective courses. These programs often lead to a degree with a professional focus, such as physical therapy, architecture, or engineering, and emphasize the skill-building necessary to fulfill the requirements for those professions. Some professional programs not only require a set of core courses but also expect students to acquire a breadth of knowledge in many fields, which will help them to be intellectually well-rounded.

Students often perceive that a liberal arts degree will not prepare them for a specific job. It is more realistic for them to consider a liberal arts education as preparation for life and a career rather than as "job training." If students have interests in a variety of subjects and want more control over their coursework, their choice of a liberal arts degree can provide the flexibility they desire. Majors in the liberal arts also may prepare students for professional or graduate programs, for example, if their career goals include pre-law, teacher certification, college teaching, or business.

Although a major in history, biology, or English may not lead directly to a specific occupation, it can prepare students for a wide range of career opportunities. Liberal arts students majoring in their favorite subject also must plan carefully for entering the workforce. To gain the broad knowledge and skills that many employers demand, they must consider taking additional courses in writing, communications, human relations, logic, computer science, or languages.

Choosing a Major

When students consider choosing a major, they might invoke the "chicken and egg" question: "Which should I choose first—an occupation, and then determine what majors might lead to that work, or should I choose a major and then figure out what occupations are relevant?" Either approach is legitimate. If you cannot decide on a career field right away but you know what academic subjects interest you, consider making the educational decision first. On the other hand, you might be able to decide on a general career direction, such as business, but you might not be sure of the major that will best lead you where you want to go.

Some students decide on a career field for which a very specific education is required, such as nursing, electrical engineering, or teaching. The educational and occupational decision is the same for them, and they can easily select their majors. Most four-year programs allow students to question and test their first decision. If they take the general education requirements that provide a base of coursework, they can later choose almost any major.

In a survey by the U.S. Department of Labor, 50 percent of college graduates indicated that their jobs were closely related to their college majors. The figures ranged from 13 percent of history majors to 92 percent in nursing. Only 57 percent of engineering graduates were in closely related jobs; 31 percent said their jobs were somewhat related to their majors.

When you select a major, ask yourself: "Does this major reflect a careful analysis of my academic strengths, limitations, interests, values, experiences, and other characteristics that make me a unique person? Am I aware of the different paths within this general career field?" For example, if you are interested in business, do you picture yourself becoming an entrepreneur, working for a large corporation, working in the public sector, or holding a job in a bank? Exercise 4.3 is designed for you to match your interests to the college majors that apply.

Different majors may prepare students for the same occupational area. Business, journalism, communications, and English majors all offer good preparation for a public relations position. A physics or history major may lead to a public relations job, too, if one's preparation includes courses in writing and marketing. Your related work experiences, leadership qualities, or demonstrated talent in the skills needed for the job you seek may be just as important to an employer as your actual degree or major.

EXERCISE 4.3   Exploring Majors

Using the information you collected in Chapter Two, you can now examine the list of majors in the matrix and consider those that reflect the Holland types that you think best describe you. The circled dot represents the *first* letter of the Holland code for that particular major (e.g., the code for Accounting is CSI).

There are two ways to read the matrix: you can start with your Holland type and identify those of interest to you, OR you can check the majors that interest you and then check out the Holland code:

_____ **1.** At the top of the matrix, **circle** two Holland types that you **think** fit you best. (Remember that these are only ideas since you may take the *Self Directed Search* to more accurately determine your Holland code [www.self-directed-search.com]).

_____ **2.** As you read down the column you circled (e.g., Social), place an "x" in the box with a dot if the major to the left sounds interesting to you. Repeat this for the second Holland type you circled.

_____ **3.** After completing the two lists, go back to your majors of interest and read across to find any that have two or more marked with your "x." These majors might be worth exploring.

_____ **4.** Place a check mark in the left column beside the majors you wish to explore in more depth.

OR

_____ **1.** Read down the list of majors, and place a check mark in the left column for any that interest you.

_____ **2.** Read across to see the Holland types represented by that major, paying particular attention to the circled dot that indicates the predominant type.

_____ **3.** Compare this with the results reflected in the exercises in Chapter Two, and determine if you might want to consider this major for further study.

College majors and related interests

Check here if you wish to explore this major further	College Major	Realistic	Investigative	Artistic	Social	Enterprising	Conventional
	Accounting		•		•		⊙
	Administration, Business				•	⊙	•
	Administration, Education			•	•	⊙	
	Advertising			•	•	⊙	
	Aeronautical Engineering	•	⊙		•		
	Agriculture	⊙	•		•		
	Ag Economics		⊙		•		•
	Ag Engineering	⊙	•			•	
	Agronomy	•	⊙		•		
	Animal Science	⊙	•		•		
	Anthropology	•	⊙	•			
	Architecture	•		⊙		•	
	Art, General Fine Arts			⊙	•	•	

(continued)

Check here if you wish to explore this major further	College Major	Holland Types					
		Realistic	Investigative	Artistic	Social	Enterprising	Conventional
	Art Education			•	⊙	•	
	Astronomy		⊙		•	•	
	Biology	•	⊙			•	
	Botany	•	⊙		•		
	Cell Biology	•	⊙			•	
	Ceramic Engineering	⊙	•		•		
	Ceramics	•		⊙		•	
	Chemical Engineering	•	⊙			•	
	Chemistry	•	⊙			•	
	Child Development			•	⊙	•	
	Chinese			•	⊙	•	
	Classics			•	⊙	•	
	Clothing and Textiles			•	•	⊙	
	Communications			•	•	⊙	
	Computer/Info Science	⊙	•			•	
	Consumer Economics		•		•	⊙	
	Criminology	•	⊙				•
	Dance	•		⊙	•		
	Dental Hygiene	•				⊙	•
	Dentistry	•	⊙		•		
	Dietetics		•		⊙	•	
	Earth Sciences	•	⊙			•	
	Economics		⊙		•		•
	Education, Elementary			•	⊙	•	
	Education, Secondary (depends on subject)		•	•	⊙		
	Engineering	⊙	•				•
	English		•	•	⊙	•	
	Environmental Science	•	⊙			•	
	Fashion Merchandising			•	•	⊙	
	Finance		•			•	⊙
	Fine Arts			⊙	•	•	
	Food Sciences and Tech	•	⊙				•
	Foreign Languages		•	•	⊙		
	Forestry	⊙	•				•
	French		•	•	⊙		
	Genetics	•	⊙			•	

(continued)

Check here if you wish to explore this major further	College Major	Holland Types					
		Realistic	Investigative	Artistic	Social	Enterprising	Conventional
	Geography	•	◉			•	
	Geology	•	◉			•	•
	German		•	•	◉		
	Health Education		•		◉		•
	History		•		◉	•	
	Horticulture	•	◉			•	
	Insurance				•	◉	•
	Interior Design			◉	•	•	
	Islamic Studies		•	◉	•		
	Journalism			◉	•	•	
	Landscape Architecture	•	•	◉			
	Library Science			•	◉	•	
	Linguistics		◉	•	•		
	Marketing				•	◉	•
	Mathematics	•	◉			•	
	Mechanical Engineering	◉	•			•	
	Medicine	•	◉		•		
	Medical Technologist	•	◉			•	
	Music			◉	•	•	
	Natural Resources Management	•	•			◉	
	Nursing		•		◉	•	
	Nutrition		◉	•	•		
	Occupational Therapy	•			◉	•	
	Oceanography	•	◉				•
	Optometry	•	◉		•		
	Parks and Recreation Management				•	◉	•
	Pharmacy	•	◉			•	
	Philosophy		◉	•		•	
	Physical Education			•	◉	•	
	Physical Therapy	•			◉	•	
	Physics	•	◉			•	
	Political Science		•		•	◉	
	Psychology		•		◉	•	
	Public Relations			•	•	◉	•
	Real Estate				•	◉	•
	Recreation				◉	•	•

(continued)

Check here if you wish to explore this major further	College Major	Realistic	Investigative	Artistic	Social	Enterprising	Conventional
					Holland Types		
	Religious Studies			•	⊙	•	
	Russian		•	•	⊙		
	Slavic Studies		•	⊙	•		
	Social Work		•	•	⊙		
	Spanish		•	•	⊙		
	Special Education		•	•	⊙		
	Speech and Hearing Therapy		•		⊙	•	
	Statistics	•	⊙				•
	Veterinary Medicine	•	⊙		•		
	Wildlife Management	•	•			⊙	
	Zoology	•	⊙			•	

What majors that you identified from the preceding exercise seem compatible with your results (i.e., Holland types) in Chapter Two?

_____
_____
_____
_____

Are these the same majors you have already considered? If so, what are they? Did you find any new ideas for majors that might interest you? If so, which ones?

_____
_____
_____
_____

The list of majors provided in this exercise is limited. (Your college's Web site or career services office will have your college's list of majors, and your career services office may have them organized by Holland codes.) Write down any other majors that you would like to add to the list.

_____
_____
_____
_____

Of all the majors you have identified, select one or two that you would like to explore in more depth.

_____
_____
_____
_____

To answer the questions in Exercise 4.4, interview faculty members, academic advisors, seniors in these majors, or others on campus who are knowledgeable about course requirements, special features of this major, possible career relationships, and other relevant information. (Keep in mind the interview tips you learned in Chapter Three, p. 33.)

EXERCISE 4.4   Researching a Major

Academic Major Interview

Name of academic major _____

Department/College _____

Name and title of interviewee _____

1. What *basic or general education courses* are required in this major (e.g., English, math, science, humanities, social science)?

   _____
   _____
   _____
   _____

2. What *basic courses in the major* can you take to test your interest/abilities in this area?

   _____
   _____
   _____
   _____

3. What are some *upper-level courses in this major* that sound interesting to you? (Give course number and name.)

   _____
   _____
   _____
   _____

4. What *additional courses* (e.g., perhaps in other departments) do you need to complete this major?

   _____
   _____
   _____
   _____

5. If *elective* hours are available in this major, what are some courses you might consider?

   _____
   _____
   _____
   _____

6. What is the *total number* of credit hours needed to graduate with this major?_____
   Number of credit hours in the major only _____

7. What is *required to enter* this major (e.g., certain courses completed, application to a selective admission area, certain grade point average; no requirements)?

   _____
   _____
   _____
   _____

8. What *occupational or career relationships* exist for this major (e.g., accounting majors can become Certified Public Accounts; English majors can become editors or teachers; consumer affairs majors can work in business; engineering technology majors can work in industry)?

_____

_____

_____

_____

9. What are some *positive* aspects of this major, according to your interviewee? Negative aspects?

_____

_____

_____

_____

10. What are your *overall impressions* of this major as a potential choice for you? If positive, what are your next steps?

_____

_____

_____

_____

Academic Major Interview

Name of academic major _____

Department/College _____

Name and title of interviewee _____

1. What *basic or general education courses* are required in this major (e.g., English, math, science, humanities, social science)?

_____

_____

_____

_____

2. What *basic courses in the major* can you take to test your interest/abilities in this area?

_____

_____

_____

_____

3. What are some *upper-level courses in this major* that sound interesting to you? (Give course number and name.)

_____

_____

_____

_____

4. What *additional courses* (e.g., perhaps in other departments) do you need to complete this major?

_____

_____

_____

_____

5. If *elective* hours are available in this major, what are some courses you might consider?

_____

_____

_____

_____

6. What is the *total number* of credit hours needed to graduate with this major? _____

   Number of credit hours in the major only _____

7. What is *required to enter* this major (e.g., certain courses completed, application to a selective admission area, certain grade point average; no requirements)?

_____

_____

_____

_____

8. What *occupational or career relationships* exist for this major (e.g., accounting majors can become Certified Public Accounts; English majors can become editors or teachers; consumer affairs majors can work in business; engineering technology majors can work in industry)?

_____

_____

_____

_____

9. What are some *positive* aspects of this major, according to your interviewee? *Negative* aspects?

_____

_____

_____

_____

10. What are your *overall impressions* of this major as a potential choice for you? If positive, what are your next steps?

_____

_____

_____

_____

Graduate or Professional Education

It may be worthwhile to consider extending your schooling beyond an undergraduate degree. Certain professions require extended education (e.g., medicine, actuarial science, law, licensed psychologist). As mentioned earlier, a graduate degree in some areas can open new or broader opportunities—for example, a Masters in Business Administration (MBA) and a Masters in Allied Health (MS). When considering graduate or professional school, examine your occupational goals, your academic abilities (as established by your academic record), your chances of being accepted by a graduate or professional school, and other personal factors such as your financial situation, family obligations, time constraints, or the need for geographical change.

A great deal of study and thought must go into such an important decision, and it is imperative to establish an exploratory plan to gather the information needed to make a realistic assessment. First, talk to faculty in your field of interest about the application process, excellent schools in that field, and your chances of being accepted. Look up possible universities on the

Internet for more information. Some computerized career information systems such as *Discover* contain information about graduate and professional programs in universities across the country. In addition, talk to individuals in the field; they will provide a different perspective about the necessity or feasibility of considering a graduate program.

After narrowing your choices to certain institutions, search on the Web or write to them for information about admission criteria and possible financial aid programs. Certain national examinations, such as the Graduate Record Examination (GRE), Law School Admission Test (LSAT), Graduate Management Admissions Test (GMAT) may be required. Explore the need for further information about credentials, licenses, and other certification requirements in certain occupations. In some cases, continuing education may be required, but not through a graduate degree.

The *Occupational Outlook Handbook* (2008–2009) has organized the fastest-growing occupations by the level of education required (see Table 4.1). What level of education is indicated for some of the occupations you are now considering? Are any of the occupations in Table 4.1 on your list? If so, which ones?

Table 4.1 Fastest Growing Occupations and Occupations Projected to Have the Largest Numerical Increases in Employment Between 2006 and 2016, by Level of Postsecondary Education or Training

	Fastest Growing Occupations	Occupations Having the Largest Numerical Job Growth
First-Professional Degree		
	Veterinarians	Physicians and surgeons
	Pharmacists	Lawyers
	Chiropractors	Pharmacists
	Physicians and surgeons	Veterinarians
	Optometrists	Dentists
Doctoral Degree		
	Postsecondary teachers	Postsecondary teachers
	Computer and information scientists, research	Clinical, counseling, and school psychologists
	Medical scientists, except epidemiologists	Medical scientists, except epidemiologists
	Biochemists and biophysicists	Computer and information scientists, research
	Clinical, counseling, and school psychologists	Biochemists and biophysicists
Master's Degree		
	Mental health counselors	Clergy
	Mental health and substance abuse social workers	Physical therapists
	Marriage and family counselors	Mental health and substance abuse social workers
	Physical therapists	Educational, vocational, and school counselors
	Physician assistants	Rehabilitation counselors
Bachelor's or Higher Degree, Plus Work Experience		
	Actuaries	Management analysts
	Education administrators, preschool and child care center/program	Financial managers
	Management analysts	Computer and information systems managers
	Training and development specialists	Medical and health services managers
	Public relations managers	Training and development specialists

(continued)

	Table 4.1 (Continued)	
	Fastest Growing Occupations	**Occupations Having the Largest Numerical Job Growth**
Bachelor's Degree		
	Network systems and data communications analysts	Computer software engineers, applications
	Computer software engineers, applications	Accountants and auditors
	Personal financial advisors	Business operations specialists, all other
	Substance abuse and behavioral disorder counselors	Elementary schoolteachers, except special education
	Financial analysts	Computer systems analysts
Associate Degree		
	Veterinary technologists and technicians	Registered nurses
	Physical therapist assistant	Computer support specialists
	Dental hygienists	Paralegals and legal assistants
	Environmental science and protection technicians, including health	Dental hygienists
	Cardiovascular technologists and technicians	Legal secretaries
Postsecondary Vocational Award		
	Makeup artists, theatrical and performance	Nursing aides, orderlies, and attendants
	Skin care specialists	Preschool teachers, except special education
	Manicurists and pedicurists	Automotive service technicians and mechanics
	Fitness trainers and aerobics instructors	Licensed practical and licensed vocational nurses
	Preschool teachers, except special education	Hairdressers, hairstylists, and cosmetologists
Work Experience in a Related Occupation		
	Sales representatives, services, all other	Executive secretaries and administrative assistants
	Gaming managers	Sales representatives, services, all other
	Gaming supervisors	Sales representatives, wholesale and manufacturing, except technical and scientific products
	Aircraft cargo handling supervisors	First-line supervisors/managers of food preparation and serving workers
	Self-enrichment education teachers	First-line supervisors/managers of office and administrative support workers
Long-Term On-the-Job Training		
	Audio and video equipment technicians	Carpenters
	Interpreters and translators	Cooks, restaurant
	Athletes and sports competitors	Police and sheriff

Source: Occupational Outlook Handbook, 2008–2009.

Distance Learning

Some students, particularly those with full-time jobs or other responsibilities, find it difficult to attend college in the traditional way. Distance education offers an opportunity for students who want to enroll in college but who cannot attend traditional classes on campus because of time, place, or other restrictions. Distance learning brings the classroom to the student rather than the student to the classroom. Teachers and students from different geographical locations can share information by e-mail, CD-ROM, cable television, audiographic teleconferencing, interactive satellite broadcasts, video conferencing and video imaging, or the Internet. Students may be at home, work, a library, or any predetermined location. The instructor may be located on campus.

Credit and non-credit courses, workshops, seminars, and continuing education can all be offered at a distance. If you find it difficult to attend traditional classes on campus because of work, family, or other responsibilities, you may want to explore the distance learning opportunities in your area. (An example of a website that offers a database of distance learning courses is www.petersons.com/distancelearning.)

Experiential Learning

You can gain important career-related learning experiences in other ways, too. Some of these are described briefly below.

EXTRACURRICULAR ACTIVITIES   Students have abundant opportunities to be involved in a wealth of campus activities. Student government, theatrical productions, choirs or glee clubs, residence hall councils, interest clubs, political action groups, and preprofessional organizations can offer students the opportunity to learn new skills, as well as to sharpen their managerial and leadership talents. Extracurricular activities also provide a forum for students from diverse backgrounds and cultures to learn from one another and appreciate common interests and goals. Colleges and universities offer a variety of artistic performances and engage speakers on myriad subjects. All these opportunities can add breadth and depth to students' general knowledge.

WORK EXPERIENCES   In Chapter Three we discussed work experiences as one source of occupational information. The knowledge you gain from work experiences also can be useful in choosing a major. Many students work part-time during college to help pay their expenses. Your work experience can also benefit your education. You can ask co-workers about their educational background and obtain information about which academic majors are necessary or desirable for certain types of work. Some part-time or summer jobs may not require a formal education, but others do. For example, if you work as a ticket taker at an amusement park during the summer, you may want to talk to the park's business managers (if you are thinking of a business major), park designers (if you are thinking of a landscape architecture or design major), or the people who keep the park running (if you are thinking of an engineering or technical degree).

In almost any work environment you also will find occupations that do not require specific academic preparation. Some business managers, for example, have a liberal arts degree and majored in English, chemistry, psychology, or French. Employers often do not focus on what your college major has been. They are looking for well-educated, well-rounded individuals who will work well in the specific job they seek to fill.

When you talk with co-workers about their educational backgrounds, you might ask them what college courses they feel were most useful for and applicable to their current work. In addition to educational insights, you can gain in any work setting the opportunity to observe how people work, test problem-solving skills, develop time-management skills, and learn responsibility and self-discipline. Work experiences also can measure your ability to get along with others and help you identify and clarify the educational and work values that are important to you.

In Chapter Seven you will apply work experiences you have had to the job-search process.

INTERNSHIPS AND COOPERATIVE EDUCATION   One of the best ways to reinforce or confirm your choice of college major is to work as an intern in an area related to your academic interests. Internships may be paid or unpaid and usually are limited to a single experience, although sometimes they may be repeated. A short-term internship is a way to gain experience in several occupational areas.

The process of applying for an internship is an excellent learning tool. Putting together a resume and interviewing for the position can be good training for a job search. If you can obtain an internship in the same city as your college, you might be able to take a lighter load of courses. The specific internship you want, however, may be located in a different geographical area. Consult with your financial aid office or other possible funding sources to see if you are eligible for a stipend. You also might obtain course credit for the experience if it relates to your academic major. You might want to check with your college to see if they subscribe to www.internshipsusa.com that lists national internships.

Co-operative experiences are different from internships in that they alternate an academic term with a term of paid, full-time employment. Some co-ops require a two-term, separate work commitment, although you may wish to voluntarily extend the number of terms in which you work in a co-op setting. Many companies offer co-op opportunities for the purpose of training future workers, and they may expect to make an incremental increase in the responsibilities your job entails with each additional term. A co-op position can offer you invaluable insights into how a work environment operates and how you can contribute to the mission of the work setting. A co-op experience is probably the best preparation for the job-search process because it provides you with firsthand experience in the field. Companies frequently hire co-op students who have graduated because the hiring personnel are familiar with the quality of the student's performance.

STUDY ABROAD   An excellent way to broaden your knowledge of and appreciation for other cultures is to take advantage of study-abroad programs that most colleges offer. You can earn academic credit for your time away, and you are exposed to new experiences. If you major in international studies, foreign languages, literature, and other humanities, you may benefit the most academically, but regardless of your major, you will return home with knowledge and memories that will last a lifetime. When you enter the job market, you will be an attractive candidate to employers who appreciate the value of exposure to other cultures and look favorably upon this unique experience.

VOLUNTEER WORK   If you are unable to take advantage of study abroad, internships, or co-ops, volunteer work will provide similar exposure in a real-world setting and will help you confirm your educational choices. Many campuses have offices with lists of volunteer sites. The Internet is another source for locating types of work experiences that align with your career goals, such as www.volunteermatch.org or www.USAJOBS.gov. Some organizations, such as hospitals and nursing homes, have volunteer opportunities. Your career services office may have a list of local volunteer opportunities.

> David is a television station manager who started as a volunteer—moving sets, running for coffee, and performing any "gofer" job asked of him. In time, he became such an accepted part of the staff that he was offered a part-time, paying job. David was able to confirm his interest in the communications area not only as a major but also a career. He later took an entry-level position, and eventually a managerial post.

SERVICE LEARNING   Some colleges incorporate service projects into curricular or extracurricular activities. Although not new (some campuses have been using service learning for more than 20 years), learning by performing service to the campus or greater community has increased in recent years. Service learning is different from volunteering in that service learning projects are designed, supervised, and evaluated based on specific educational goals. Service projects might include service within the campus, the immediate community, or the wider community. They may be incorporated as a curricular requirement or as an academic credit course. If your campus offers service learning as an option, you may not only offer service to others or gain practical knowledge and experience but also may be able to connect your involvement to work-related activities that you can use later in the job search process.

While the various types of experiences described (extracurricular activities, work experiences, internships, cooperative education, study abroad, volunteer work, and service learning) will help you make more satisfying educational choices, they also will also give you insights into potential career areas. Academic interests and early life experiences frequently stimulate interests in related occupations.

Furthermore, the amount of preparation needed for occupations such as physician, lawyer, engineer, and college professor is extensive. Are you willing to commit the time and effort required to achieve your goal? Clearly, your educational decisions are an integral part of choosing your career.

CASE STUDIES

Exploring

JED

It never occurred to Jed that he would not go to college since his family always assumed he would. When he checked the reasons for attending college in Chapter Five, he realized many of his reasons were personal and career related rather than academic. When he checked the majors within the Holland types of Social and Realistic, he found very few that overlap. He realized that his ideas about coaching and being a personal trainer actually involved activities and work tasks that fit both profiles. He decided to keep marketing as an option since it still interested him. He decided to interview academic advisors and faculty members in these departments. Since he had already interviewed a teacher and personal fitness trainer, he decided to use the alumni bank offered by his college to talk to people who work in these fields. He also found out more about the internships that were available in these areas.

MARIA

Maria found that she had a strong interest in computer science and other business majors. This helped reinforce her ideas about learning to be a computer programmer, but she decided to explore the different educational and training options needed in this field. Since computer-related jobs were often in the business world, she decided to explore other business-related majors, such as finance and real estate. She was both excited and scared, since she was not sure she could do it. Did it make sense for her to embark on a difficult course of study when she had so many responsibilities? How would college affect her work and family life? She had many factors to consider as she debated her options. ■

Summary Checklist

WHAT I HAVE LEARNED

____ After examining my college's list of academic majors, I have narrowed them down to at least two.

____ I have examined these majors in view of my interests and abilities and have confirmed that they are realistic.

____ I have talked to faculty and departmental academic advisors and/or seniors in these majors and know exactly what curricular requirements are necessary to complete a degree in these areas.

HOW I CAN USE IT

I can relate academic majors to specific career areas but I know that one major may lead to many jobs, many majors may lead to one job, and some jobs require no specific major.

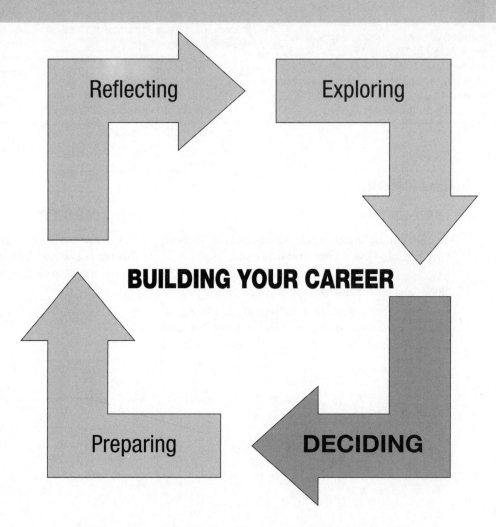

CHAPTER 5

Reflecting

Exploring

BUILDING YOUR CAREER

Preparing

DECIDING

"Adults always ask little kids what they want to do when they grow up because they are looking for ideas."

PAULA POUNDSTONE

The preceding chapters in this book have (1) introduced you to the career planning process, (2) helped you explore your career-related personal characteristics, (3) helped you conduct occupational information searches, and (4) helped you explore educational alternatives. It is now time to make some decisions based on the information you have gathered during this process. But first you will gather insights into your own unique decision-making attitudes and style and how you can apply this knowledge to making the most realistic and satisfying career choices.

FACTORS IN DECISION MAKING

Every day we make decisions. Some, such as getting up in the morning, are so automatic that we give them little thought. Others, such as buying a car, are more important and require a great deal of research, reflection, and study. Career decisions obviously call for careful thought and planning. Although everyone approaches the career decision-making process differently, you must take into account certain factors if the process is to be effective and satisfying for you. Exercise 5.1 requires your input to discover how you make decisions.

EXERCISE 5.1   How I Make Decisions

Read the following sample decisions and consider how you would make each one (or how you made it in the past). Some might call for more than one letter.

- Put "O" if *others* make the decision for you.
- Put "R" if the decision is so *routine* you don't even think about it.
- Put "T" if the decision requires occasional *thought.*
- Put "D" if the decision requires a lot of thought and is *difficult* to make.

SAMPLE DECISIONS   **HOW I MAKE DECISIONS**

1. When to get up in the morning _____
2. What to do when I have free time _____
3. To tell the truth _____
4. To disagree strongly with a friend _____
5. What to wear _____
6. To drive faster than the speed limit _____
7. To go to a party instead of studying _____
8. To cope with a serious family problem _____
9. To make an occupational choice _____
10. To finance my education _____
11. To attend classes _____
12. What courses to select _____
13. What major to choose _____
14. To seek help with personal problems _____

Did this activity offer insights into the way you make decisions? If so, what were they?

_____
_____
_____
_____
_____

How did you mark items 9 and 13? Why?

_____
_____
_____
_____
_____

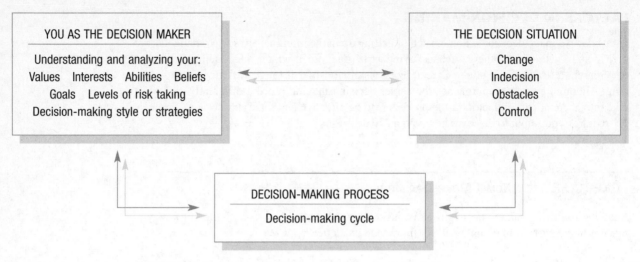

FIGURE 5.1   Dimensions of decision making.

Dimensions of Decision Making

There is more to decision making than you may realize. Three basic components are especially important:

1. You as the *decision* maker
2. The *decision situation*
3. The decision-making *process*

Figure 5.1 depicts the interaction among these three parts which we will discuss in detail next. Making decisions without considering your personal values, attitudes, and other important characteristics that make you unique will likely yield an unsatisfactory outcome. Also, each decision situation is different. You behave differently when deciding what clothes to buy than when you are choosing a major. The decision-making process consists of a logical progression of steps and tasks.

Myself as Decision Maker

As the decision maker, the first consideration should be your personal characteristics—values, interests, aptitudes, and skills—that you identified in Chapter Two. Your beliefs and feelings also influence your decisions. Knowing yourself is critical to career decision making and will lead to a productive, satisfying career that will reflect your strongest interests, aptitudes, and values.

In Chapter Two you identified your work values. These will influence your thinking as you begin to establish career and life goals. For example, if finding an occupation that involves working with people is important to you, you need to incorporate this work value into your decision-making deliberations. Simply identifying your values isn't enough. You also have to integrate them into the process. Exercises 5.2 and 5.3 will help you identify your values and how to incorporate them in your decision making.

EXERCISE 5.2   Identifying My Values

In Chapter Two you identified your work values. It is often difficult, however, to identify your most fundamental personal and life values. This exercise might put the process into perspective and reveal the important link between you and your values. Imagine that you are 90 years old and a reporter from the local newspaper has requested an interview with you. The newspaper wants to write a feature article about you and what you accomplished during your lifetime. Write a headline for the article about yourself. (You also may want to write the article itself!)

_____

_____

_____

What does the headline tell you about your values or what is important to you in life?

_____

_____

_____

EXERCISE 5.3   **Using My Career Values in Decision Making**

Review your personal work values from Exercise 2.4 in Chapter Two and write them on the lines below. Would you like to change any of them at this time? Add or change some if you wish.

_____

_____

_____

Are these work values the same or compatible with those in your headline? (If they are very different, you may want to clarify what is really important to you.)

_____

_____

_____

Review the other personal information you gathered in Chapter Two. What are your strengths (strongest skills and aptitudes)?

_____

_____

_____

What are your limitations?

_____

_____

_____

RISK TAKING

Being a decision maker entails an ability or willingness to take risks. For example, you may be willing to take a risk during a card game with friends because the consequences are not going to affect your life. In a more important situation, such as how long to study for a final examination, you may be less willing to take a risk. When you make a decision, consider how much you are willing to risk, taking into account the possible good and bad consequences of the decision. For example, if you decide to buy a used car instead of a new one, you may save money, but you may have larger repair bills later. Exercise 5.4 asks you to determine whether you are or are not a risk taker.

EXERCISE 5.4   **Am I a Risk Taker?**

Think about your capacity for risk taking and mark an "x" in the place on each line that best reflects where you rate yourself for that situation.

NO RISK	TO DISAGREE STRONGLY WITH YOUR BOSS	HIGH RISK
NO RISK	TO KEEP AS A PET A MONGREL DOG YOU FOUND ON THE STREET	HIGH RISK
NO RISK	TO DRIVE BEYOND THE SPEED LIMIT	HIGH RISK
NO RISK	TO JOIN THE MILITARY	HIGH RISK
NO RISK	TO CHOOSE AN ACADEMIC MAJOR	HIGH RISK
NO RISK	TO SEEK HELP CONCERNING PERSONAL PROBLEMS	HIGH RISK
NO RISK	TO CHOOSE AN OCCUPATION	HIGH RISK

Give examples of situations in which you would be willing to take a risk.

_____

_____

_____

Give examples of situations in which you would not be willing to take a risk.

_____

_____

_____

In your opinion, are you a *high, medium* or *low* risk taker? _____

How did you mark the amount of risk you would take in choosing an academic major and occupation? What does this tell you about your approach to making these decisions?

_____

_____

_____

_____

PERSONAL DECISION-MAKING STYLE

Your personal style of decision making refers to *your approach in making decisions*. Figure 5.2 depicts the information-gathering and analysis dimensions of decision making. Researchers Johnson and Coscarelli suggest that some people may be more *spontaneous* in this process while others are more *systematic*. A spontaneous person makes a quick, intuitive decision and later tests it against information. A systematic decision maker, by contrast, feels more comfortable gathering a lot of information before making a decision and is often slower to make a commitment.

In analyzing information once it has been gathered, the *external* decision maker likes to think aloud and enjoys discussing the decision situation with friends, family, a counselor, or others before deciding. The *internal* decision maker needs to think about the information before talking to anyone about it.

When we combine these two dimensions of information gathering and analysis, we identify four distinct decision-making styles: spontaneous external, spontaneous internal, systematic external, and systematic internal. Identifying and understanding your style will help you become a more effective decision maker. For example, if you tend to be more spontaneous and external in making decisions, you probably will enjoy assignments that require talking to people in various occupations. You will engage in brainstorming and group discussions, review decisions with a classmate, or jump readily into volunteer or work experiences to test your ideas. If you tend to be more systematic and internal, you probably will enjoy reading descriptions of people in various careers; organizing your ideas in a summary grid, carefully considering the pros and cons of each alternative you identify; or using computerized career information systems to gather information in an organized way.

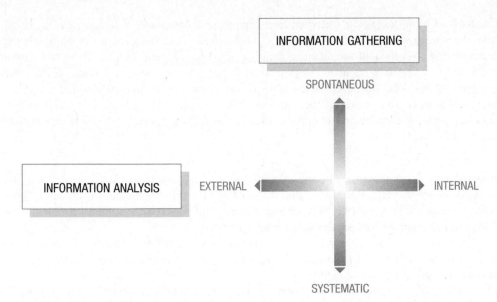

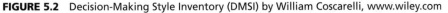

FIGURE 5.2   Decision-Making Style Inventory (DMSI) by William Coscarelli, www.wiley.com

A number of the activities in this book ask you to respond in a systematic way; however, spontaneous decision makers will benefit from them as well. In fact, spontaneous decision makers often use systematic methods when making certain decisions. On the other hand, people with a systematic style may be uncomfortable with spontaneous methods such as class discussions, but they will benefit from hearing other students' spontaneous responses to their ideas. Exercise 5.5 is designed to elicit your decision-making style.

EXERCISE 5.5   **My Decision-Making Style**

Think about the approach you use when making important decisions:

I make decisions spontaneously because it feels right.	_____ yes	_____ no
I make decisions systematically because I prefer to have information before I weigh alternatives.	_____ yes	_____ no
I prefer to talk to people whose judgment I trust before deciding. *(externally)*	_____ yes	_____ no
I prefer to think about a decision before I discuss it. *(internally)*	_____ yes	_____ no

Discuss why you have chosen each dimension and how your style might have influenced your past educational and career decisions.

_____

_____

_____

_____

If you would like to examine your decision-making style in more depth, ask your instructor for a copy of the Decision Making Style Inventory (DMSI). More information is available at www.decisionmakingstyleinventory.blogspot.com.

The Decision Situation

The decision situation incorporates the environment in which the decision is being made and all the factors involved. Sometimes you have control over elements or factors in a decision situation and other times you do not. The factors relevant to almost every decision-making situation are change, indecision, obstacles, and control.

CHANGE   Change can occur when you least expect it and complicate a decision-making situation. It can happen before, during, or after you have made a decision, and it can even alter the outcome of a well-thought-out, planned decision. For example, you may decide to buy a used computer after you have compared its price with that of other new and used machines and after you have obtained the financing. When you call to purchase the computer, you find that it has been sold already. Your action has been thwarted (or changed) even though your original decision was sound. Expecting and adapting to change are skills we need to learn, because change is often beyond our control.

INDECISION   Even though gathering information, generating alternatives, and weighing the evidence may help you reduce indecision, those efforts do not eliminate indecision entirely. A certain amount of uncertainty is to be expected in most situations, but when indecisiveness turns into procrastination, or even paralysis, it can be debilitating.

Anxiety is part of being indecisive. A little anxiety is probably helpful as it forces us to take action we might not otherwise take. Doing nothing about uncertainty may only lead to more anxiety and sometimes to lost opportunities.

When you feel uncertain about a decision, it is best to become involved in some productive activity, such as information gathering. For example, when you are deciding among two or three career choices, you might collect information about all three (e.g., by talking with workers in the field, volunteering or obtaining work experiences, or reading about those occupations) and then weighing the pros and cons.

OBSTACLES   You inevitably will encounter obstacles in most decision-making situations. These obstacles can be internal (of your own making) or external (those that other people or circumstances place in the situation). Exercise 5.6 is a checklist of frequent obstacles.

EXERCISE 5.6   Checklist of Obstacles

Below is a checklist of obstacles that people frequently encounter. Check (✓) those you may be facing as you attempt to make a tentative career decision.

INTERNAL OBSTACLES	EXTERNAL OBSTACLES
_____ Fear of failure	_____ Family career pressures
_____ Lack of motivation	_____ Poor job market when I graduate
_____ Fear of making the wrong choice	_____ Societal barriers, (e.g., discrimination)
_____ Lack of confidence in my skills	_____ The academic major I need is not available at my college
_____ Eliminating certain occupations because of stereotypes I hold	_____ Lack of money to pursue education and training

What other internal or external obstacles might you encounter? How would you overcome them?

_____

_____

_____

_____

_____

CONTROL Who is in control of your career decisions? You may be tempted at times to make decisions based on someone else's wishes or desires. Although it may be easier to allow others to make decisions for you, if you depend on others for answers, you might not get the results you want. Decision makers must live with the outcomes of their choices, so they must ensure that the final decision is theirs alone. For example, if you chose premedicine as your major because your parents pressured you, but you dislike the coursework, you might resist changing majors because you feel you are letting them down.

The pressure to select a career quickly can be strong at times, but indecision about your career is not a sign of weakness. Taking some time to explore can be a positive activity that leads to a stable, satisfying decision. Feeling independent and in control is a prerequisite to effective decision making.

The Decision-Making Process

The better you understand your strengths and limitations as a decision maker in a variety of situations, the easier the decision-making process will be for you. Figure 5.3 illustrates a decision-making cycle that takes a systematic approach. Each step in this cycle is described below.

DEFINING THE PROBLEM Although the critical first step in the decision-making process should be obvious, it is often ignored. First, *define what you are trying to decide.* For example, rather than trying to tackle your occupational choice all at once, break it down into its components. Rather than asking, "In what career will I spend my life?" define the problem more specifically: "What groups of occupations offer the best opportunity for me to use my love of sports?" Name the problem in specific terms. Stating the problem as a question helps to define it.

STATING YOUR GOALS Next, state your goals. Your future expectations as they relate to your decision will influence the way you approach the other steps in the cycle. If your long-term goal, for example, is to find a job in which you can be a professional person, work for yourself, and make a high salary, you will have narrowed down considerably the information you gather and the alternatives you identify.

Setting goals is one of the most important steps in the decision-making process, as it involves projecting your values into the future. It also requires clear and critical thinking. Goal setting is a way of establishing early what you hope to accomplish by the end of the decision-making process.

Once you have made a decision (see Step 5 of Figure 5.3), check your goals and values to see if your choice has fulfilled them. If so, you are ready to take action.

Note that the vertical arrows point both ways in the cycle. Sometimes the information we collect after setting our goals (Step 3) points to directions other than those we initially considered. If this occurs, you may have to reformulate your goals in light of new or different information. In fact, your career and life goals are continually subject to change as you, your needs, or your situation changes.

Some important factors involved in goal setting are listed below. As you begin to formulate your personal and work-related goals, keep these principles in mind:

1. *Be sure that your goals are your own.*   You are more likely to accomplish personal and career goals that you set for yourself than goals that others set for you.
2. *Write down your goals as clearly and concisely as possible.*   Writing down your goals will make them real and available for you to review. Make a genuine commitment to strive for your goals.
3. *Begin with simple, short-term goals.*   Starting with short-term and attainable goals will help you gain confidence and experience in goal setting.
4. *Consider your values as you set goals.*   Goals are values projected into the future. Goal setting is easier if you clarify your values.
5. *Be sure that your goals are attainable.*   Your goals should be realistic and represent a reasonable objective toward which you are willing and able to work.

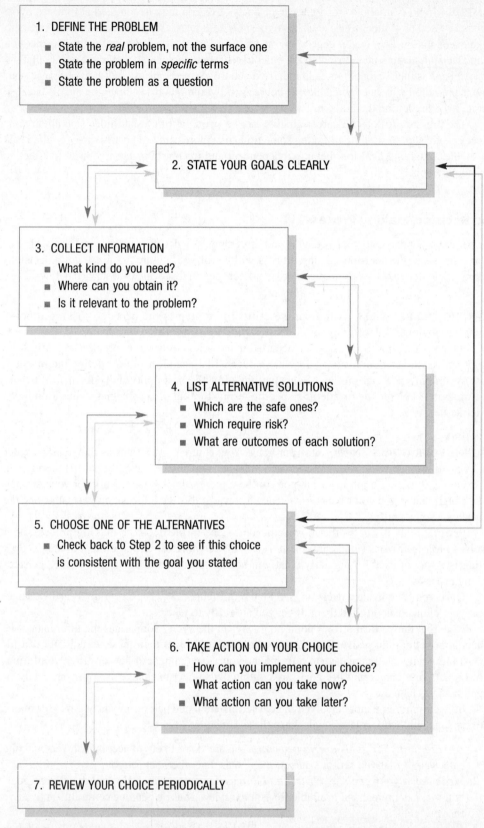

FIGURE 5.3   The decision-making cycle.

6. ***Set time limits for obtaining your goals.***   Specifying a certain date for a goal to be accomplished will help you stay motivated and reinforce your efforts to attain it. Dates and times can and should be flexible, however, so you can change them when necessary.

You are encouraged to write your goals in Exercise 5.7.

EXERCISE 5.7	**What Are My Goals?**

Write down a school-related, short-term goal you wish to accomplish in the next several months.

_____

_____

_____

Write down a career-related, short-term goal you wish to accomplish in the next year.

_____

_____

_____

Write down a career-related, long-term goal you wish to accomplish in the next five years.

_____

_____

_____

Now examine the goals you recorded above, using the following criteria:

1. *Is my goal stated in specific terms?* (If not, rewrite it.)
   (Examples: "I want to get good grades this semester" is too general. A more specific goal is: "I want to get at least a B in chemistry this semester" or "I want to obtain a job in sales before I graduate.")

2. *Is my goal attainable?*
   - Is there enough time to accomplish the goal?
   - Am I responsible, or are there conditions beyond my control?
   - Do I have the knowledge and abilities to accomplish the goal?
   - Am I motivated enough to carry the goal to completion?
   - Do I believe in the goal?
   - Is the goal compatible with my values?

3. *How will I know when I have fulfilled my goal?*
   - What are some tangible signs?
   - What will I have accomplished?

   Goal setting is important in any decision-making situation, but it is especially critical in the career decision-making process.

COLLECTING INFORMATION   After you have identified the decision and stated your goals, you will have to collect a great deal of information about your area of interest. You already have gathered information about your personal qualities and occupational and educational options, in Chapters Two, Three, and Four. What other information do you need? Where can you find it? Who can help you?

LISTING ALTERNATIVE SOLUTIONS   At this point, you should have before you many alternatives. For example, if you have collected information about professions that allow you to work for yourself and make a high salary, you may have identified medicine, law, or accounting, among others. If you examine the information you have gathered about yourself, which of the alternatives best fits your interests and abilities? Which alternatives reflect your work values? What are possible outcomes or consequences of each alternative? As you begin to integrate your self-knowledge and occupational information, you can narrow down and eliminate some of your choices. Exercise 5.8 is provided for that purpose.

EXERCISE 5.8   Identifying Alternatives

Below, write the three possible occupational alternatives identified in Exercise 3.2 in Chapter Three. List the pros and cons of each alternative.

	PROS	CONS
ALTERNATIVE 1	_____	_____
	_____	_____
	_____	_____
	_____	_____
ALTERNATIVE 2	_____	_____
	_____	_____
	_____	_____
	_____	_____
ALTERNATIVE 3	_____	_____
	_____	_____
	_____	_____
	_____	_____

Which of your alternatives seems to be the best occupational choice?

_____

CHOOSING ONE OF THE ALTERNATIVES   By now one alternative may stand out so that you are ready to make a decision. Is this choice consistent with the goals you set for yourself in Step #2? Now is the time to consider the risk factors and obstacles that may prevent you from carrying out the decision.

Name of major and/or occupation I have decided upon:

_____   _____

Use this checklist to confirm your choice(s). Circle yes or no.

yes   no   This choice matches my interests as identified in Chapter Two.
yes   no   I have the abilities needed for this choice.
yes   no   This choice incorporates my work values.
yes   no   My personality seems compatible with this choice (as suggested by the Holland types discussed in Chapter Two).
yes   no   The coursework required for this choice is interesting to me.
yes   no   I have a good chance of making good grades in classes related to my choice.
yes   no   My chances of finding a job in this field are good.
yes   no   I am willing to take risks that might be associated with this choice.
yes   no   This choice will lead me to the goals I stated earlier in this chapter.

Have you answered "yes" to all the statements above? Are you ready to decide?

My choice of major and/or occupation(s) is (are):

_____   _____

Now you can proceed to the next step in the decision-making process. If you are ready, skip ahead to the section called "Taking Action on the Choice."

If you are *not* ready to make a commitment, examine the reason(s) you have circled "no." If you notice too many conflicts or cannot resolve them, you may want to return to Exercise 5.8

and identify another alternative. You also may want to complete Exercise 5.9 to help you focus on a direction.

EXERCISE 5.9 Why Some People Don't Act on Their Decisions

Listed below are some reasons that people don't make a commitment to their decisions. Check (✓) those that apply to you.

_____ You have made very few important decisions on your own, so you don't know how to take action.

_____ You feel it makes no difference whether you do it or not; it is out of your control.

_____ You are concerned about what others will think; maybe they will disapprove.

_____ You don't know what action steps need to be taken, so you don't know where to begin.

_____ You have not set priorities, so you don't know what to do first.

_____ You are overwhelmed by all that needs to be done, so you don't take any action.

_____ You will put it off until someone or some event forces you to take action.

_____ You are afraid of failing. What if you have made the wrong decision or taken the wrong action?

_____ You are afraid of succeeding. If you succeed you will have to deal with what comes next.

_____ You are not willing to give up immediate gratification for long-term gain.

Have you checked any of these reasons? If so, what can you do to counter them?

_____

_____

_____

If you cannot resolve the above thoughts or behaviors, you may want to consult with your instructor or a counselor for some suggestions.

TAKING ACTION ON MY CHOICE

Once you have made a commitment to your choice, you need to take action because a decision is not finalized until you have taken action to implement it. What immediate steps can you take to set your decision in motion? (For example, if you have chosen an academic major, what do you need to do to declare this major officially?) In Exercise 5.10 you will fill out an Action Plan.

EXERCISE 5.10 Action Plan

What action will you need to take later? Devise a plan that includes action steps you will need to take in the future to implement your major and occupational choices.

Action I must take:

_____

_____

When?

_____

_____

Where?

_____

_____

How?

_____

_____

☐ Check when complete.

_____

From the above plan, what action do you need to take first? How will you prioritize the action steps in terms of importance rather than timing? Now that you have committed to a decision and have an action plan, you will need to be aware of the last step in the decision-making process: to review your choice periodically.

REVIEWING YOUR CHOICE PERIODICALLY   You will need to reevaluate all your decisions on an ongoing basis. Anticipated and unanticipated changes may alter your thinking. Sometimes personal situations will force you to reconsider your ideas about work or your desired lifestyle. Accept change. Don't be afraid to change or try to anticipate change and guide it. Keep in mind your capacity to take risks. You will want to reevaluate your original decision based on actual rather than projected outcomes.

Once you have made a decision, taken action, and reviewed it, you face a series of new decisions. If you choose to become an attorney, for example, you will need to decide on a major, plan when to take the national law test (LSAT), and consider how you will pay for law school, where you wish to practice, and so forth. Exercise 5.11 may help you in decision making.

Conceptualizing decision making as a cycle will help you manage a complicated process in an orderly, rational, and timely way. As you saw in Figure 5.2, the arrows between steps go both ways. You will need to reevaluate or recycle your decision-making efforts at certain stages. If the alternative solutions you identified are not possible or desirable, you will have to collect more information and generate new alternatives. You may even have to restate your goals or redefine the decision itself in different or simpler terms.

In this chapter, you have moved through the decision-making cycle by completing the exercises. Where do you think you are in the cycle of choosing a major or a career field?

EXERCISE 5.11   **Making Decisions**

We have discussed many aspects and dimensions of the decision-making process. Think for a few moments about how you make decisions. How have you made decisions in the past?

_____

_____

_____

_____

How will you approach career decision making now?

_____

_____

_____

_____

What is different? What is the same?

_____

_____

_____

_____

What resources (e.g., friends, parents, counselors, library, workers) do you have to help you?

_____

_____

_____

_____

You now have identified your personal qualities, generated occupational and educational alternatives, and learned the factors involved in complex decisions. In Chapter Six you will learn about the future work place and how it might affect your decisions.

CASE STUDIES

Deciding

JED

JED is quite aware that he is not a good decision-maker. Every time he is faced with making an important decision, such as choosing an academic major, he procrastinates until people or circumstances force him to choose. He has vowed, however, that he will select an academic major by the middle of his sophomore year. Jed knows he is not a risk taker and learned in Chapter Five that he is more systematic than spontaneous in the way he approaches decisions. He also admits that he relies on other people's opinions too much, as opposed to taking responsibility for making decisions himself.

When Jed weighs the pros and cons of the choices he has considered before and during this course, majoring in physical education seems the strongest. Teaching and coaching would allow him to work with children, which he enjoys, and give him the foundation to return to school to take more academic work in any area relating to fitness if he desires. As part of his action plan, Jed learned the requirements for entering the education major at his college. His back-up plan is to major in marketing, and he is taking courses that will fulfill the requirements of both majors.

MARIA

Maria believes her decision making has improved since she graduated from high school. Although she tends to be spontaneous in making decisions, working and rearing a child have resulted in her taking time and being more systematic about the decisions she makes. In thinking about what she wants to do, Maria has weighed many alternatives. She knows she is motivated and is gaining more confidence in herself as a result of actually enrolling in a college class. Maria doesn't want to do anything that will interfere with her current job success, but she realizes she must obtain new skills if she is to be financially stable.

Although finding the money for college will be a challenge, Maria does plan to seek tuition reimbursement from her employer. Her mother and father have encouraged her and have offered to take care of her daughter while Maria attends evening classes. Maria knows she has never been a risk-taker, but she realizes that now may be the time to find the courage to be one. ■

Summary Checklist

WHAT I HAVE LEARNED

_____ Decision making is a process in which I am constantly engaged.

_____ I have compared how I have made decisions in the past with the dimensions described in the chapter and have a better understanding of myself as a decision maker, how the decision situation presents different challenges, and how the decision-making cycle works.

_____ Having engaged in the decision-making process in this chapter, I now am able to specify at least one major or occupation that would be satisfying to me.

HOW I CAN USE IT

I will be able to use the decision-making skills I have learned or strengthened in this chapter to make career choices in the future.

How Can I Prepare for the Future Workplace?

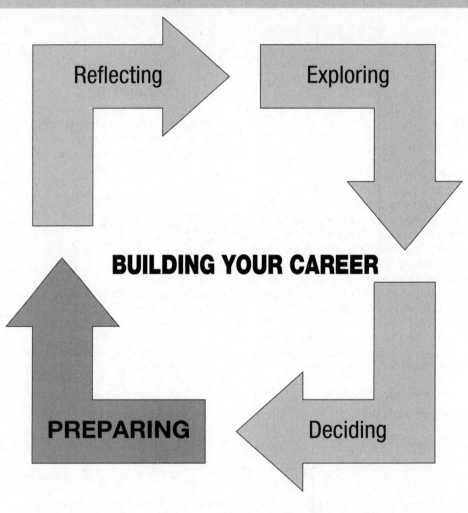

"I look to the future because that is where I am going to spend the rest of my life."

GEORGE BURNS

In the preceding chapters you identified several occupational fields that you explored in depth. An important aspect of gathering information about occupations is to learn about the future job outlook and the projected growth of these occupations by using the U.S. Department of Labor and other futurist sites. In this chapter you will learn how to access this information, and through your research you may be able to confirm your current ideas or add more occupations to your list. Also in this chapter you will learn about the future workplace and how you can prepare to succeed in it.

An important aspect of building your career is to be aware of the impact that the future workplace will have on your daily work and personal life. Not only are work environments and the workforce undergoing change, but even work itself is being transformed. According to the U.S. Bureau of Labor Statistics, you can expect to have more than eleven different jobs between the ages of eighteen and forty-two. How can you prepare now for a work life that will need to evolve in an ever-changing work world? What personal qualities and skills will you need to develop in order to be ready? The first task is to understand the general factors precipitating this change and how they might affect your career decision making. In this chapter you will learn about:

- the important factors changing the workplace,
- workplace trends that might influence your job search,
- employment projections and other trends, and
- the skills and personal qualities you will need to be successful in the future workplace.

WHAT FACTORS ARE INFLUENCING THE PRESENT AND FUTURE WORKPLACE?

The most important factors influencing the future workplace, according to futurists, are shifting demographic patterns, globalization, and accelerated technological change.

EXERCISE 6.1   You and the Future Workplace

The future workforce will shift toward a more balanced distribution by age, gender, and race/ethnicity. Not only will the demographic profile of the workforce change considerably, the number of people with disabilities is rising, and many Americans will be faced with balancing work and a multigenerational family.

Question: How well do you work with diverse groups of people, including those from a generation other than your own? How can you improve your communication and relational skills to work more effectively with diverse co-workers and supervisors?

_____

_____

_____

_____

Globalization has created a growing market for goods and services, and many new types of mobile populations are forming. The global economy has been greatly influenced by information technology. Rapid and inexpensive ways to communicate, plus the more rapid transfer of knowledge and technologies has spawned new ways to do business. As you work in an increasingly global work world, you will need new knowledge and skills that include expertise in languages and familiarity with other cultures.

Question: Are you prepared to live in a global workplace? Regardless of your major, do you know about geography, history, languages, and other cultures? Have you studied a semester in another country? What can you do in college to increase your knowledge and experiences of people from other parts of the world?

_____

_____

_____

_____

Technological advances are so common today that we take them for granted. Not only do advances in information technology affect our work life, but the accelerating pace of that change challenges even the most adept worker. Social networking (such as LinkedIn, Facebook, and YouTube) is having a serious impact on the workplace. Laptops, cell phones, and the Internet have altered wherever and whenever work is performed.

Question: How do you rate your computer skills and other technical knowledge? What can you do while in college to improve, expand, and learn new technological skills?

_____

_____

_____

_____

WHAT DO I KNOW ABOUT WORKPLACE AND HIRING TRENDS FOR THE NEXT 5 TO 10 YEARS?

One interesting way of keeping up with the trends in the workplace is to look at job titles. Some of you will hold jobs in the future that don't even exist today. Have you ever heard of a Vice-President of Experiences, a Telemedicine Technician, a General Manager of an Underwater Hotel, a Computer–Human Interaction Technician, or a Skycar Mechanic? Gioia and Herman (2005) indicate that trends in technology, society, demographics, and the economy will inspire the job titles of tomorrow. Some old jobs will change in name only. New names will be given to critical positions in order to attract applicants (e.g., sewer workers have been reclassified as subterranean engineers). New jobs will develop in response to shifts in the marketplace or advancing technologies. Many workers will become more mobile. Some will carry their office in their pocket and work when it is convenient for them and their clients. The U.S. Department of Labor reports that the number of Americans who work remotely (e.g., from home) has increased dramatically.

Other trends according to the Department of Labor include increased self-employment; compensation not only by money but also by other forms of social exchange (e.g., barter or "time dollars"); hiring of more freelance or contract workers; and more reliance on skills such as creativity, flexibility, and responsibility. In the future, careers and their related college majors will become more specialized. New college majors are created as a result of new career fields. For example, rather than majoring in business, more students are exploring specialized majors such as sustainable business, strategic intelligence, and entrepreneurship.

Are you interested in "green jobs"? The green economy has the promise of many new types of occupations and is reshaping many old ones. The Department of Labor describes three types of green jobs:

1. those where there will be more demand for the work activities and technologies of jobs that already exist (e.g., architectural drafters, chemists, computer software engineers, hydrologists, and wildlife biologists);
2. those where the shape of the work tasks and worker requirements, including job performance, will be "enhanced" (e.g., architects, atmospheric or space scientists, energy crop farmers, solar energy engineers, wind turbine electrical engineers, and environmental journalists); and
3. those that will require unique work tasks and worker requirements in new and emerging occupations (e.g., air-quality control specialists, automotive engineers, climate change analysts, and carbon credit traders). If you have an interest in jobs related to the greening economy, you might want to explore this important trend through the Department of Labor's Web site (www.dol.gov). A search for "green jobs" will provide links to many sites about this area.

Workforce Trends

Tomorrow's workforce, as stated earlier, will look very different from those of the past. According to the Department of Labor, workers will be older. The baby-boomer generation has been the major force in the labor market for over 20 years. Many boomers are reaching their prime working years while others are beginning to retire. Generation X (those born from 1961 to 1981) and the Millennials (those born from 1962 to 2000) will dominate the workforce in the next decades. According to the Department of Labor, more young people are working. The typical young person held an average of nine jobs between the ages of 18 and 32, with more than half of the job changes occurring before age 23.

Another important influence on the future labor market will be the population changes in race and ethnicity. Immigration will add even more diversity to the American workforce. The number of women in the workforce has more than doubled since 1967, and the percentage of women now working is equal to the percentage of men. (This does not mean women are moving into more prestigious jobs or making as much money as men, however. The work many women do is more "recession proof," or more resistent to layoffs during downturns in the economy.) The educational attainment of the American worker is rising. Not only are more Americans graduating from high school (83 percent) but more are going to college. So the trend for the composition of the workforce in the future is a shift toward a more balanced distribution by age, sex, race, and ethnicity, and workers will be better educated than in the past.

For more information about these and other trends, go to the Department of Labor's Web site (www.dol.gov) and search for "Futurework—Trends and Challenges for Work in the 21st Century."

Employment Projections

If you are wondering where you can find accurate projections of the jobs that will be needed in the future, the most reliable source is the U.S. Department of Labor. The Bureau of Labor Statistics examines the relationships between the nation's population, the labor force, and the demand for goods and services. As a result it publishes its best estimates of future job growth and demands. You can discover occupational areas with positive growth opportunities by reviewing the Department of Labor's charts and reports. For example, Chart 6.1 depicts the department's projections for the fastest-growing occupations from 2008–2018.

Occupations	Percent change	Number of new jobs (in thousands)	Wages (May 2008 median)	Education/training category
Biomedical engineers	72	11.6	$ 77,400	Bachelor's degree
Network systems and data communications analysts	53	155.8	71,100	Bachelor's degree
Home health aides	50	460.9	20,460	Short-term on-the-job training
Personal and home care aides	46	375.8	19,180	Short-term on-the-job training
Financial examiners	41	11.1	70,930	Bachelor's degree
Medical scientists, except epidemiologists	40	44.2	72,590	Doctoral degree
Physician assistants	39	29.2	81,230	Master's degree
Skin care specialists	38	14.7	28,730	Postsecondary vocational award
Biochemists and biophysicists	37	8.7	82,840	Doctoral degree
Athletic trainers	37	6.0	39,640	Bachelor's degree
Physical therapist aides	36	16.7	23,760	Short-term on-the-job training
Dental hygienists	36	62.9	66,570	Associate degree
Veterinary technologists and technicians	36	28.5	28,900	Associate degree
Dental assistants	36	105.6	32,380	Moderate-term on-the-job training
Computer software engineers, applications	34	175.1	85,430	Bachelor's degree
Medical assistants	34	163.9	28,300	Moderate-term on-the-job training
Physical therapist assistants	33	21.2	46,140	Associate degree
Veterinarians	33	19.7	79,050	First professional degree
Self-enrichment education teachers	32	81.3	35,720	Work experience in a related occupation
Compliance officers, except agriculture, construction, health and safety, and transportation	31	80.8	48,890	Long-term on-the-job training

SOURCE: BLS Occupational Employment Statistics and Division of Occupational Outlook

CHART 6.1 Fastest Growing Occupations.

Of the twenty fastest growing occupations in the economy, shown in Chart 6.1, half are related to healthcare. The aging of the baby-boom generation has resulted in rapid growth in health care occupations. Chart 6.1 also provides information on current wages as well as the education and training needed to prepare for these fast growing occupations.

If you wish to explore many facets of specific occupations, you may want to use the U.S. Department of Labor's classifications of ten *occupational groups*. Occupations frequently are grouped together based on the tasks that workers perform. One advantage of grouping occupations is to make it easier to show employment trends that require similar skills. The ten groups and the work tasks they perform are these:

1. *Management, business, and financial operations:*   Workers in this group plan and direct the activities of business and government. Examples of occupations include managers in advertising, public relations, marketing, human resources, finance, purchasing, and education. Others are accountants, budget analysts, insurance underwriters, farmers, ranchers, and agricultural managers.

2. *Professional and related occupations:*   Workers in this group include a wide variety of skilled professions. Examples of occupations include computer scientists, mathematicians, engineers, chemists, lawyers, teachers, graphic designers, athletes, interpreters, opticians, dentists, physical therapists, and various other health technologists and technicians.

3. *Service occupations:*   Duties of service workers cover a wide range of jobs from cooking and serving meals to fighting fires. Examples include firefighters, chefs, home health care aides, pharmacy aides, nursing aides, correctional officers, child care workers, and maintenance workers.

4. *Sales and related occupations:*   Workers in this area sell goods and services. Examples include cashiers, insurance sales agents, real estate brokers, and travel agents. The occupation in this group where growth will be highest is retail salesperson.

5. *Office and administrative support occupations:*   Workers in this group perform the daily activities of offices, deal with the public, distribute information, and include bill and account collectors, billing and posting clerks, payroll clerks, tellers, customer service representatives, secretaries, interviewers, library assistants, meter readers, and postal clerks.

6. *Farming, fishing, and forestry:*   Workers in this occupational group cultivate plants, breed and raise livestock, and catch animals. Examples of occupations are fishers, fishing vessel operators, agricultural workers, and conservation and logging workers.

7. *Construction and extraction occupations:*   Construction and extraction workers build new residential and commercial buildings and also work in mines, quarries, and oil and gas fields. Occupations include home and commercial builders, brick masons, carpenters, building inspectors, electricians, roofers, painters, and hazardous materials removal workers.

8. *Installation, maintenance, and repair:*   Workers in this group install, maintain, and repair equipment. Occupations in this group include auto service technicians, mechanics, electrical and electronic installers and repairers, aircraft mechanics, heating and air-conditioning mechanics and installers, and millwrights.

9. *Production occupations:*   Production workers assemble goods and operate plants and factories. Metalworkers, food processors, woodworkers, plastic workers, assemblers and fabricators, and textile occupations are included in this group.

10. *Transportation and material moving occupations:*   Workers in this area transport people and materials by land, sea, or air. Occupations include truckers and movers.

The percent change in employment by major occupational groups from 2008–2018 is shown in Chart 6.2. Professional and related occupations, which includes a wide variety of skilled professions, is expected to be the fastest growing major occupational group, at 17 percent, and is projected to add the most new jobs—about 5.2 million. The occupations in this group require at least a bachelor's degree and some require additional graduate coursework or degrees.

To learn more about these ten occupational groups, and the occupations within each, complete Exercise 6.2, where you will search the *Occupational Outlook Handbook* (www.bls.gov/oco) for specific occupations that interest you.

Percent change in total employment by major occupational group, 2008-2018 (projected)

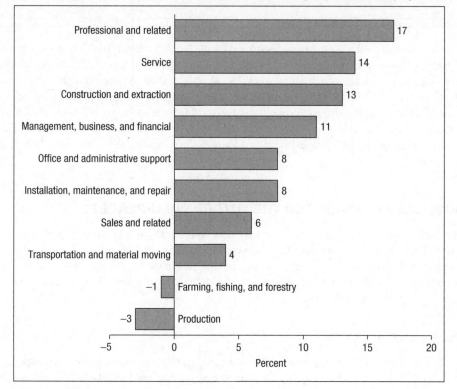

CHART 6.2   Change by Occupational Group.

EXERCISE 6.2	Searching for Job Outlook and Projection Data

____ **1.** Enter the *Occupational Outlook Handbook Web site* at www.bls.gov/oco.

____ **2.** Select one of the occupations you identified on page 27 in Chapter 3.

____ **3.** Type the name of the occupation in the "Search" box in the upper right corner.

____ **4.** Select the occupational title on the resulting screen (there will be a list of similar occupations from which to choose).

____ **5.** In the list under the occupation's title, click on "Job Outlook" for information about the employment growth expected for this occupation.

____ **6.** Click on "Projections Data" for information about the projected employment for this field to 2016.

____ **7.** You will also find the latest "Wage Information" for this occupation and "Related Occupations" that lists occupations similar to this one.

For example, the employment growth for *psychologists* through 2016 is expected to be faster than average, and projected employment is expected to increase by 15%. Annual earnings for a psychologist range from $45,300 to $102,730, depending on specialty and experience.

What did you discover about the future of the occupation that you just researched?

_____

_____

_____

_____

What is your reaction to this information? How can you use it?

_____

_____

_____
_____
_____

Caution: Never make a career decision based on today's "hot jobs." They may not be hot tomorrow. Economic and other social circumstances could (and have!) drastically changed or reversed job prospects in just about every occupational area. At one time, for example, telephone operators and IBM punch card operators were among the "hot jobs." Although knowledge of demographics and job projections is useful information, good advice could turn bad tomorrow. The Internet is rife with sites that tout the "next hot jobs." Consult reputable sources, such as the U.S. Department of Labor, before making decisions based on "the next best thing."

HOW CAN I PREPARE FOR THE FUTURE WORKPLACE?

What are some personal steps you can take now to prepare for this constantly changing workplace? The college years are the time to develop the personal habits, attitudes, and skills to make yourself more marketable. It is also the time to take part in the experiences and activities that are available on and off campus. You will find some suggestions for enhancing and developing your personal qualities and skills below.

Career and Life Skills

In Chapter 2 you assessed the work skills that the U.S. government indicates are essential in the work world today. In their book *21st Century Skills,* Trilling and Fandel (2009) list some life and career skills that will be essential for the future worker. As you read these skill descriptions, assess your strengths in these areas.

EXERCISE 6.3   How Ready Am I?

Flexibility and adaptability: I can be flexible and adapt well to new and unexpected changes in my academic and other work situations.

/_____/_____/
Very flexible   Somewhat flexible   Inflexible

Initiative and self-direction: When I work, I take the initiative and am self-motivated and self-directed.

/_____/_____/
Very self-directed   Somewhat self-directed   Rely on others for direction

Social and cross-cultural skills: I have strong social skills and can work well with co-workers from different cultures and with beliefs different from my own.

/_____/_____/
I work well with people   I usually work well with   I have difficulty working
different from me.   people different from me.   with people different
                                                                from me.

Productivity and accountability: I am productive in the use of my time and other resources and accountable for details when I work.

/_____/_____/

I am always productive	I am usually productive	I have difficulty in always
and accountable.	and accountable.	being productive and
		accountable.

Leadership and responsibility: I have demonstrated leadership qualities and take responsibility for the success of any work I do.

/_____/_____/

I am a strong leader in	I am a strong leader in	I do not like to be a
most situations.	some situations.	leader and never take
		that role.

As you consider how you assessed these career and life skills you now possess, how ready are you for the future work world? Which skills do you need to work on? What specific steps can you take to acquire or expand each of these skills (e.g., take classes about other cultures, join a student organization to practice leadership and social skills, take part in an internship experience to test initiative and adaptability)?

_____

_____

_____

_____

_____

_____

_____

The following action steps suggested by Lombardo (2006) offer a way to develop a future orientation and help you test your readiness for preparing for your future in both your personal and work life:

- Challenge existing habitual beliefs about the future.
- Brainstorm about alternative visions and beliefs about the future.
- Clarify and assess your life plans and goals, and imaginatively and critically consider alternative possibilities.
- Learn about history and especially long-term trends that are continuing in the present.
- Learn the practices and techniques for enhancing thinking skills, visualization, imagination, and creativity.

Some people find that projecting themselves into the future is difficult. Many college students in particular don't take the time to think about themselves in the five or ten years after college. Setting goals that far ahead may seem like an impossible task, but many decisions made during the college years will have a direct impact on entry-level jobs that are available to an individual after graduation. Being aware of what is happening in your career field and keeping track of work trends and projections may influence your consideration of certain academic choices and experiences. Thinking and acting like a futurist might make a difference in the way you identify academic and vocational alternatives and might open up new and exciting opportunities that you never knew existed.

CASE STUDIES

Preparing

JED

Jed was surprised that he hadn't thought much about the job outlook for the fields he was considering. He wondered about the difference in job prospects for teaching and becoming a fitness trainer. His research indicated that the job outlook for teachers was expected to grow about 12% or "faster than average" by 2016. Job prospects for the future of teachers overall varied from "good to excellent," depending on the subject and level of teaching and location. Job prospects were better for teachers in high demand areas such as science and bilingual education or in less desirable urban or rural school districts. When he searched the outlook for fitness workers, he found the need for fitness trainers was expected to rise faster than average at 27%, and—as for teaching—the pay range depended on the type of fitness-related occupation and the place of employment. Jed realized that he needed to do more research about these occupations since it raised many new questions for him.

MARIA

Maria had always assumed that any job in the computer field was secure. Her research confirmed her thinking that technology was a growing area with many different job opportunities. She discovered that many more occupations than she was aware of incorporated computer knowledge and skills. When she searched for job outlook and projection data for computer programmers, however, she found that the outlook for this occupation is expected to decline slowly to 2016. Many reasons were given for this decline, including outsourcing and the ability of many to design, write, and implement their own programs. Maria began to explore other occupations in the computer field by using the list under "Related Occupations." She found that computer scientists and database administrators, for example, will advance much faster than average—about 37%. As a result of finding this information, Maria decided to explore other computer-related occupations while keeping her original idea of becoming a programmer. ■

Summary Checklist

WHAT I HAVE LEARNED

_____ I know now the importance of thinking about the future workplace as I engage in career decision making.

_____ I know how and where to obtain information about future work trends and employment projections.

_____ I have a better understanding of the skills and personal qualities that will be necessary to be successful in the future workplace.

HOW I CAN USE IT

I can now add information about future job possibilities to what I learned in Chapter Three. I will continue to stay current on trends and future employment opportunities in my career field as I progress in my major. I know I need to improve my goal setting skills for my immediate and long-term future.

How Will I Advance My Career?
The Job Search and Résumé Writing

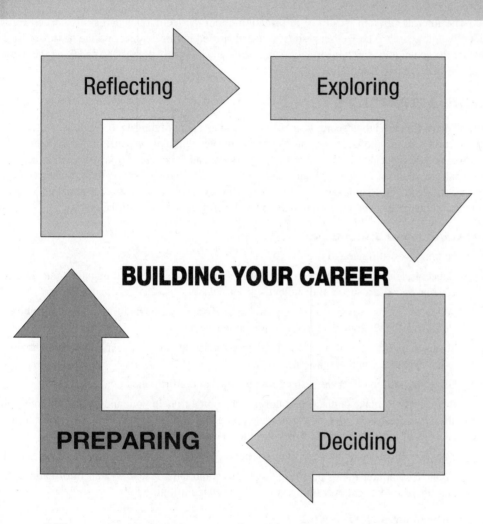

"When you are asked if you can do a job, tell 'em, 'Certainly I can!'
Then get busy and find out how to do it."

THEODORE ROOSEVELT

SELLING YOURSELF

In previous chapters you learned about your personal strengths and how they might fit into different academic and career fields. This chapter focuses on the skills you will need to continue the career planning tasks that will ultimately help you obtain your ideal job. Whether you are about to seek your first "real" job, or another in a series, you can benefit from learning and practicing the skills needed to mount an effective job search. Because experts project that you probably will change jobs many times during your life, once you learn these skills, you will be able to use them throughout your career.

The job-search process can be both exhilarating and difficult. You will need to plan carefully, with determination, flexibility, and an honest appraisal of who you are and where you are going. Selling yourself is not a comfortable prospect for everyone, but to succeed you must believe in your ability to be an exceptional contributor to an organization and be prepared to market yourself with that attitude and belief. The main prerequisites are to know your strengths, know what you want, and be willing to spend the time and energy to enter the search process with knowledge and enthusiasm.

Ample help is available for you to learn the skills required to mount a productive job search. Many colleges have career planning and placement services that can help you develop specific job-search tools. Once you have started your search, you can seek the guidance of campus experts about how to write a résumé, become an effective interviewer, follow up after an interview, and manage job offers.

The Internet offers a wealth of information about the techniques and skills needed for a productive job search. Many other resources are identified in this chapter and the next. But first, consider the actual job-search information and skills you currently possess by checking the items under the Action Steps that follow.

TAKING ACTION STEPS

Some students wait until their senior year before they think about finding a job. Actually, you should begin to build your résumé as a freshman. Picturing how you will look on paper in two, four, or more years will help you decide the kind of knowledge, skills, and experiences you will need to acquire during college. In this way, you are taking control of your future by beginning to formulate a career plan that will lead you to graduation and beyond. The following action steps are arranged by academic year. Later in this chapter, you will learn how to accomplish many of these tasks.

What Can First-Year Students Do?

Check the items you still need to do.

_____ Concentrate on learning how to study, write papers, take tests, and manage your time so you can become a successful student.

_____ Scope out campus activities (e.g., student government, intramural sports, symphonic choir) that match your interests, and join at least one.

_____ Select courses wisely, using the help of your academic advisor to explore possible majors or confirm one you have chosen.

_____ Use informational interviews to choose a major or confirm one.

_____ Begin early to make contacts and develop a résumé to help you land a good summer job after your freshman year, or if you are employed full-time, think about how you can improve your job or how it matches your long-term career goals.

_____ Expand your computer literacy by taking courses to learn or to improve your skills in this area.

_____ Create a computer file or purchase large folder and label it "Job Search Information." In that file or folder, put everything you collect related to future jobs.

What Can Sophomores Do?

_____ Confirm your choice of major or seek help in changing to one that is better suited to your interests and abilities.

_____ Register with your campus career services office.

_____ Volunteer for jobs or positions in campus organizations that can help you acquire organizational, managerial, and leadership skills.

_____ Attend career days and job fairs to gather information about career fields that interest you.

_____ Take advantage of your campus career-planning resources, such as testing services, computerized career information systems, career library, and career counseling.

_____ Enroll in a career-planning course if you are still not certain about your major or career direction (unless you are already in one).

_____ Begin thinking of people whom you might ask to give you references, such as faculty or employers.

_____ Look for part-time or summer jobs that can provide work experiences to help you confirm your major and/or career choice.

_____ Begin to find out about co-op or internship possibilities for your junior or senior year.

_____ Continue to place in your "Job Search Information" file the information you are collecting.

What Can Juniors Do?

_____ Register with your career services office if you have not already done so.

_____ Update your résumé.

_____ Conduct informational interviews in the career field you are considering.

_____ Begin to build a network of contacts in your field.

_____ Sign up for résumé-writing workshops; take a workshop to practice interviewing techniques.

_____ Establish a credential file in your career services office if offered; continue to collect letters of recommendation from faculty and others.

_____ Do serious research on possible employers and workplaces; use the Internet or collect lists available in your campus career services office. Ask family and friends for ideas.

_____ Seek internship or co-op placements for this year and or your senior year.

_____ Invest in appropriate interview clothes.

_____ Find a summer job in a field related to your career goal.

_____ Improve your skills in the art of job searching on the Internet.

_____ Look at job intership postings Web sites that relate to your field of interest; add them in your "Job Search Information" file along with other job descriptions you have been collecting.

What Can Seniors Do?

_____ Register with your campus career services office if you have not already done so.

_____ Take part in an internship or co-op experience, if available.

_____ Expand and refine your list of contacts.

_____ Examine what you have collected in your job search file and make contacts with the persons or companies that have job possibilities.

_____ Update your résumé; have it reproduced professionally.

_____ Create an electronic scannable résumé in addition to your paper version.

_____ Invest in appropriate interview clothes.

_____ Update the references in your credential file in the career services office or those in your own file.

_____ Interview with prospective employers through your career services office.

_____ Learn to navigate the Web for on-line job searches.

_____ Contact off-campus work sites if needed.

_____ Use your co-op or internship experience to establish your work priorities.

_____ Consider job offers and weigh each on criteria you have established (opportunities to use your knowledge and skills, freedom to be creative, opportunities for promotion, salary and benefits package, relocation flexibility, lifestyle implications, etc.)

What steps do you need to take _now_ to move further along your career and job-search path (e.g., create a job information file, set up a personal file in your campus career services office, sign up for a résumé-writing or job interviewing workshop)?

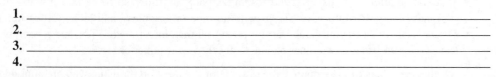

1. _____

2. _____

3. _____

4. _____

WRITING A RÉSUMÉ

Your résumé is one of the most important parts of your job search. A résumé lists your accomplishments and experiences in a way that tells employers who you are and what you can contribute to their enterprise, whether it is in business, education, government, or another type of work environment.

Your résumé is the first step in obtaining an interview. In the Internet age, many of the rules for résumé writing are changing. Because most employers look at hundreds of résumés and screen them quickly, your résumé must be impressive or it may end up in the wastebasket. Employers are often looking for key words such as *internship, proficient,* or *collaborated,* and action verbs such as *implemented, organized,* and *coordinated.* Key words are also important to employers as they scan résumés electronically. Some résumé experts suggest that a separate keyword section might improve the odds of keyword searching software selecting the résumé that matches those it is seeking.

It takes careful thought and preparation to create a résumé that presents you in the best possible light, and writing a good résumé means following a certain set of rules and using "résumé language." For example, always write in the first person, but never use the words *I* and *my;* never use the articles *a, an,* and *the;* use present tense for current activities, past tense for past experiences and activities.

Some career experts suggest that résumés should reflect the applicant's career identity or image. Rather than an objective statement, a "branding" statement at the top of the résumé promises that you can deliver what the employer is seeking. Your brand defines who you are and what benefits you can uniquely deliver to the employer. Your branded message can be projected through every word and aspect of your résumé. Many resources (e.g., books, Internet sites) are available to help you form a branding statement that will sharpen the image you wish to project in your résumé.

Résumé Formats

Although the chronological résumé format is often preferred by most employers, some individuals (such as those with no previous employment, with gaps in employment, or with frequent job changes) may prefer a functional format that emphasizes related skills or functions rather than employment. Advantages of the chronological résumé are that it has a logical flow and is easy to read. Disadvantages of the chronological format are that it highlights frequent job changes, emphasizes gaps in employment, and doesn't show skill development. The functional résumé emphasizes skills rather than employment and can organize a variety of experiences such as paid and unpaid work and other activities. Some people prefer a combination of both in order to de-emphasize employment history in jobs that are not relevant to the current job being sought but can highlight their most relevant skills and accomplishments. The intent always is to organize your résumé so the reader can find all relevant information quickly and easily.

Common Résumé Errors

A résumé that has not been carefully thought out and contains obvious errors will not be read for more than a few seconds by an employer. Figure 7.1 demonstrates some of these mistakes. The following are some common errors that can be avoided:

- *Unfocused objective.*   Make sure your objective is clearly defined. A stated objective that is too general might give the impression that you are uncommitted or unqualified for that particular position. It is best to focus on the job title for which you are applying rather than to convey a more general goal.
- *Writing not concise.*   Avoid too much straight text. Divide long paragraphs into smaller ones. Use short bullet-point phrases to make the format easier to read. Begin sentences with strong action verbs.
- *Keep the résumé as short as possible.*   One page may be enough in many cases; never use more than two pages for an entry-level position.
- *Make it readable.*   A disorganized résumé is hard to follow, so be certain it is easy to read, has plenty of white space (areas with no type or graphics), and looks professional.
- *Final check.*   Check your final draft for poor grammar, misspelled words, and typographical errors. Ask at least two other people to check your résumé for errors.

Another error is not to personalize the résumé for the position for which you are applying. Employers will look at your qualifications as they pertain to the position they are filling. Make sure your résumé tells who you are and what you can contribute specifically to that position position (i.e., your brand). Creating more than one version of your résumé gives you the opportunity to tailor the information to a specific job description. Revise goals, modify professional objectives, or rearrange work and volunteer activities to emphasize experience and skills that focus on the requirements for the specific job.

If you were an employer and received this résumé, would you hire this person? What errors are evident? (The obvious errors are listed after the résumé.)

DONALD WORD
1400 52nd Street
Oak Park, MA

<u>Career Objective:</u> To work in the business field as an intern

<u>Education:</u>

High School: Graduated from Finley High in 2010. Participated in sports.

Will graduate with a bachelors degree from Whitfield University hopefully in 2004 with a degree in business in 2014

<u>Work Experience:</u>

Donney's Pizzaria, Oak Park, MA   2012

Worked parttime in sales and later as a cook.

McGill's Department Store, Oak Park, MA   2013 to present

I worked at McGill's department store as a clerk in sporting goods. In that job I sold sporting goods such as golf, baseball, and football equipment. I was also responsible for restocking shelves. This involved taking inventory dailey. I also waited on customers and answered their questions about our merchandize.

<u>Other Work Experience:</u>

Camp counselor at Bigfoot Camp, Maine—summers of 2011

Usher at Palace Theatre, Oak Park, MA—summer of 2009

<u>Activities:</u>

Play on intermural sports teams; dorm representative; Ski Club

Computer Skills: Familar with Word Perfect, and E-mail engines.

RÉSUMÉ ERRORS:

No phone number, e-mail address, or zip
   code given
"Objective" too general
Unattractive overall appearance; difficult
   to read
Work experiences not in chronological order;
   incomplete dates
Job description too wordy; more detail needed

Overuse of "I"
Misspelled words
Verb tenses not consistent (e.g., current job
   description should be in present tense)
Computer skills incomplete

FIGURE 7.1   Flawed résumé for Donald Word.

Appearance

How your résumé looks is as important as its content. Arrange the information so it appears well-organized and professional. If you do not have access to an excellent printer, consider using those available at quick-print shops. Store a general cover letter and revise it as needed to include specific, personalized information about each prospective employer. A poorly prepared résumé or cover letter reflects poor work habits.

As stated before, poor grammar, misspellings, and other errors are unacceptable. Also, a résumé that is too fancy can distract from the central message. Avoid colored paper or paper that does not duplicate clearly, as an employer may copy your résumé many times. It is especially important to keep your résumé simple when faxing or sending it electronically. Underlining, bullets, and small type, as examples, may not be clearly reproduced.

Final Touches

When you are ready to write a final version of your résumé, you already will have completed the most difficult task of remembering and organizing the information you need. If you have not started this activity, begin now! Create a computer file or worksheet with the sections noted above, and begin to fill in the blanks with everything that comes into your mind, no matter how irrelevant it may seem at this time. Continue to record information in the file as you accumulate school experiences, work in part-time or full-time summer jobs, or in any other situation in which you are acquiring relevant knowledge and skills. Do not put anything on your résumé that you aren't prepared to elaborate on during an interview.

Computerized résumé packages are available. Your college career planning office may have a résumé software package installed, or you may want to purchase one at a computer store. These packages can provide a quality, flexible résumé development program. You can select the type of format you wish to use (chronological, skills, functional) and indicate the typestyle and any graphics you desire. Résumé programs ask specific questions relating to career objectives, work experience, and education. Your résumé will be on a disk or flash drive so you can update it easily. A disadvantage of these packages is their inflexibility.

RÉSUMÉ DISSEMINATION

There are other methods for sending your résumé to a prospective employer in addition to the usual e-mail attachment or directly to an employer's Web site. A few are described below.

Video Résumés

One approach to résumé dissemination, although it is somewhat costly, is the video résumé. Some job-search firms are asking their clients to talk about themselves on a 5- to 10-minute video. Videos offer an added dimension to the hiring process, because employers can screen prospects for an interview based on how they present themselves on the video. Some employers like video résumés because they save the company time, money, and even travel. Some employers may not care for the video résumé, so you will have to determine their attitude toward this technique before sending one. If you do decide to send a video résumé, make sure it is a professional product.

Electronic Résumés

An important approach is the electronic résumé. Placing your résumé on the Internet offers another avenue for selling yourself in a competitive market. The three basic types of electronic résumé submission are e-mail, on-line, and newsgroups.

E-mail is the most common method for electronically submitting a résumé either as an attachment or inserted as text. Some employers require you to send your résumé via this method. Most employers have Web sites with applications in which students can download their résumé. They will assume you have basic computer skills and are Web-literate. When using a newsgroup, a résumé may be loaded the same way as through e-mail.

Scannable Résumés

Employers who receive large numbers of résumés are now using computers to store them. In databases the computer scans keywords relating to the posted positions and places them in the appropriate file. Résumés collected in this way must be adjusted so they are readable. It is advisable to add a section containing the keywords from your résumé that are specifically relevant to the position for which you are applying so the computer will select it during a search. These keywords can include skills (e.g., specific computer skills), work experiences (e.g., research), or educational information (e.g., Finance major). Many résumé-scanning systems recognize nouns as opposed to verbs.

For the scannable format, résumés have to be simplified. For example, do not use graphics, highlighting, different fonts, underlining, parentheses, asterisks, or italics. Columns also will confuse the computer. No line of text should be longer than 65 characters. You may want to send a copy of your regular résumé along with a scannable version, as some employers may prefer the printed variety. Always include a cover letter.

Preparing for your future now is the key to an effective job-search campaign. Although there are no set rules for writing a résumé, your intent is to make the most favorable impression possible. Don't be modest; this is the time to emphasize your strengths.

MAINTAINING A RÉSUMÉ FILE

As previously noted, your freshman year is the time to imagine how you will look on paper in the future. It is never too early to think about the skills, education, work experiences, and personal qualities that make you a unique person.

It is extremely useful early on to create an outline or general framework for your résumé and fill in the sections as you progress through school. You will then have a running account of your experiences and accomplishments, some of which are important but easily forgotten. A sample résumé worksheet is offered below in Exercise 7.1.

EXERCISE 7.1   Sample Résumé Worksheet

Name

Your name should stand out in bold capital letters, preferably centered on the page. You may want to put both your current and permanent addresses equally spaced, if they're different. (This is especially important if your current address will change and you want to make certain an employer can reach you after a specific date.) Place your e-mail address and telephone number, including area code, at the top with your name.

Goals

Goals are what you project for yourself in the future: I want to work for a "Big Four" accounting firm; I want to work as a social worker in a hospital setting; I want to teach social studies in a high school. These phrases will be reworded later as career objectives—for example, "to obtain a position in public accounting" or "to use my skills and experiences as a social worker in a health care setting."

The goals and objectives you state on your résumé should *pertain directly to the type of job for which you are applying.* This means that you may write several versions of your résumé, depending on which objective or goal you use. Make your goals as specific as you can. Career objective statements can include the type of position you are seeking, the work environment you desire (e.g., industry, business, nonprofit, health care), and the specific skills you bring to the position.

Put yourself in the place of a prospective employer. Do your goals realistically match the job or work environment? Your goals may change over time; this is a natural phenomenon. If you rewrite your goals, continue to state them in specific terms.

State a goal or career objective here:

_____

_____

_____

Qualifications Summary

If you have a great deal of work experience, you may want to insert a summary of it after your career objective statement.

Education

Your educational intent for now may be to obtain a specific degree (for example, "My goal is to obtain a bachelor of arts degree from Utopia University with majors in English and political science"; or "My goal is to obtain a bachelor of science degree in physical therapy"; or "I am working toward a master's degree in business administration"). Write below what your educational goal is now:

_____

_____

In a résumé, of course, you will list your degree(s) in a section about your educational background. Always arrange items in reverse chronological order if there is more than one (the most recent first). If you have received any honors, such as being on the Dean's list or other academic achievements, you may want to list them in this section. Include any special training you have received or credentials you have obtained. List relevant courses you took in college if they pertain to the job you seek. Your résumé should include either an overall gradepoint average (GPA) or a GPA for courses in your major. (Some advise not putting in your GPA if it is below 3.0.) You will have to decide whether to include this information. A sample education section of a senior's résumé might look like this:

Education

B.S. in Business Administration *Lincoln University,* Ames, Minnesota. expected May 1, 2XXX, overall GPA: 3.0/4.0

Extensive course work in consumer behavior, economics, technical writing, and computer science.

Write below how you will list the items in your educational background (as you see them now):

_____

_____

_____

_____

_____

Work Experiences

You may want to place this section before the education section if your work experience is stronger. List your last place of employment with a description of your duties, followed by your other employment experience, in reverse chronological order. If you have acquired strong skills and limited work experience, you may want to consider the functional résumé format, which highlights your abilities rather than emphasizing the sequence of your work experience. Experiences that show skills or functions in certain areas (e.g., organizational, managerial, interpersonal) can be grouped together. For example, under "organizational ability," you may want to describe your responsibilities as chairperson of the student-sponsored "Career Day" committee (e.g., coordinating committee, creating an advertising campaign, arranging the physical facilities). Another approach is to summarize your skills separately, after the education section. As indicated before, internships are important and should be listed under "work experience."

Use action verbs in a résumé, as they make your work experiences appear strong. Using action verbs brings your résumé to life. For example, "supervised and trained five salespersons," or "ordered and managed stock," or "initiated and organized campuswide food drive." As mentioned before, employers who are using electronic tools are searching résumés for certain key words. A list of sample action verbs follows.

accomplished	created	interpreted	produced
achieved	delegated	investigated	projected
adapted	demonstrated	launched	proposed
administered	developed	lectured	provided
analyzed	directed	led	qualified
applied	edited	maintained	researched
arranged	established	managed	revamped
assisted	executed	motivated	revised
budgeted	expedited	negotiated	scheduled
built	forecasted	observed	set up
chaired	formulated	operated	solved
changed	generated	organized	surveyed
communicated	guided	oversaw	trained
compiled	implemented	performed	transformed
conceived	initiated	persuaded	worked
conducted	instructed	planned	wrote

Other descriptors can specify specific skills or experiences such as "Internet researcher," "Web-based marketing," or "Videotape editing."

Employers focus on your activities and achievements and, through action verbs, you are conveying what you can do for them. Emphasize your strengths, accomplishments, abilities, past experiences, qualifications, and skills. You need to impress them with your ability to work well with others, learn quickly, and analyze and solve problems. Provide specific information so your qualities are measurable. For example, being promoted from cashier to assistant manager in a fast-food restaurant indicates responsibility and leadership qualities. Being elected to an office in a student organization can also show leadership qualities. List your present position in present tense; past positions in past tense.

List your work experiences to date in reverse chronological order (the most recent first):

_____

_____

_____

If you have experiences other than work that are relevant to your objective, you may want to add a section labeled "Other Experiences" or "Additional Experiences" here.

Additional Information

You may want to include on your résumé pertinent information that does not fit into other sections, such as *Accomplishments* or *Honors,* that an employer might want to know. (For example, include (1) courses you have taken that directly relate to the job you are seeking, such as computer languages or technical writing; (2) study abroad; (3) if you have earned all or part of your college expenses; (4) membership in professional organizations; (5) being a published author; (6) leadership roles in student organizations, and (7) knowing a foreign language.) List some of your accomplishments below:

_____

_____

_____

Skill Identification

You may want to add a "skills" section to your résumé, particularly if you're applying for a position for which *specific* skills are required. In Chapter Two you assessed your interests, values and skills. Chapters Three and Six emphasized many types of work skills as critical to the future workplace. If you have developed specific skills of which you want an employer to be aware, you may want to emphasize them on your résumé. The action verbs used in relating work experiences reflect skills as well. Examples of skills might include:

initiated a project	compiled statistics
administered a program	wrote for publication
supervised others	researched on the Internet
developed software	negotiated a plan
budgeted expenses	resolved a conflict
coordinated a large event	investigated and resolved a problem
evaluated a program	

As stated in Chapter Two, we sometimes underestimate our ability to do certain tasks, even though we have the skills to accomplish them. Identifying skills in a specific section will inform a prospective employer of your marketable strengths.

When you have little work experience and are applying for an entry-level position, you may want to consider organizing your résumé by skill areas rather than chronologically. This is called a *functional résumé.* This format also may be useful to mature professionals who have a great deal of expertise or job experience in a field, individuals returning to the workforce after an extended absence, or career changers. A functional résumé does not emphasize job titles or employers but, instead, focuses on skills and abilities. It has the advantage of emphasizing an individual's specific skills for a specific position. As stated earlier, most employers prefer the traditional chronological format, however.

Personal Data

Include personal information only if it is relevant to the job or if you are willing to relocate. Do not include height, weight, marital status, hobbies, or other information that is not relevant to the job or illegal.

_____

_____

_____

References

Your references can make the difference between landing a job or not. *Be sure to obtain permission from anyone you are using as a reference!* Establish a file in your college's career services office, if that service is available. If not, keep your own file. You can ask employers, faculty, administrators, and other people who have come to know you personally to write letters of reference for your file. Request a letter of recommendation any time, as it is sometimes difficult in your senior year to obtain a recommendation from a faculty person with whom you worked as a sophomore or a junior. If you decide to go to graduate or professional school, faculty recommendations are especially important.

If you write "References upon request" in your résumé, be prepared to provide them during an interview or as requested. If your college career services office maintains a service that will send your references at your request, you will want to list its name and address. Below, list the references you have already obtained. If you have not contacted references yet, write down the names of persons you want to contact.

_____

_____

_____

Using a worksheet such as this, you can maintain a running account of what you are accomplishing during your college career. Monitoring your progress can help you fill any gaps that may emerge as you analyze how your education, campus involvement, and work experiences are helping you reach your goals.

Use Exercise 7.2 to compose the different elements in your résumé as you would write them in an actual résumé. Then write an actual résumé that is ready to be sent.

EXERCISE 7.2 **Résumé Worksheet**

My Personal Goals (Career Objectives)

_____

_____

_____

_____

_____

_____

_____

Education

_____

_____

_____

_____

_____

_____

_____

Internships

_____
_____
_____
_____

Work Experiences

_____
_____
_____
_____
_____
_____

Campus Activities

_____
_____
_____
_____
_____
_____

Volunteer

_____
_____
_____
_____

Relevant Course Work

_____
_____
_____
_____

Honors

_____
_____
_____
_____

Other Knowledge/Talents/Skills

_____
_____
_____
_____

References

_____

_____

_____

_____

_____

_____

_____

_____

Figures 7.2–7.7 are some examples of how to organize and present material. Figure 7.2 is an improved version of the résumé in Figure 7.1. The others are examples of chronological, functional and skills styles of résumés, as well as résumés for summer jobs.

Donald Word

1400 52nd Street   (209) 721-4567
Oak Park, MA 12345   dword@whitfield.edu

OBJECTIVE   Seeking a sales or marketing internship

EDUCATION   Whitfield University, Waverly, MA
                     Bachelor of Science, Business Administration, May, 2014
                     GPA: 3.20
                     Self-financing 80% of college expenses

EXPERIENCE   **McGill's Department Store,** Oak Park, MA

                     Sales person, December, 2013 – present

                     • Sell sporting goods, such as golf, soccer, baseball, and football
                       equipment
                     • Respond to customers' questions about pricing and selection
                     • Inventory equipment daily and stock shelves
                     • Receive customer payments and balance cash drawer daily

                     Donney's Pizzeria, Oak Park, MA

                     Cook, May – August, 2012

                     • Received phone orders from customers, accurately recorded them
                     • Promoted to cook after six weeks

                     Bigfoot Camp, Shady Hill, ME

                     Camp Counselor, Summer, 2011

                     • Assisted with activities for a group of six 10-year-old boys
                     • Planned weekly group meetings and team activities

                     Palace Theater, Oak Park, MA

                     Usher, Summer, 2009

                     • Received tickets from customers and directed to theaters
                     • Assisted disabled customers in getting to their theater
                     • Cleaned theaters after each showing

ACTIVITIES   • President, Ski Club
                     • Residence Hall floor representative
                     • Whitfield University intramural basketball and baseball

COMPUTER SKILLS Microsoft Word, Excel, PowerPoint

FIGURE 7.2 Improved résumé for Donald Word.

DENNIS DOE

30 Raspberry Road, Columbus, Ohio 43213
614-924-3456 • doe.9@liv.edu

Professional Objective

To obtain a position as an account executive in the public relations field

Key Word Summary

Leadership, internship, Web marketing

Education

Bachelor of Science, Lincoln University, Columbus, Ohio

Expected June 2XXX, Bachelor of Science in Business Administration

Major in marketing, minor in English; extensive course work in consumer behavior, economics, technical writing, computer science, GPA 3.5/4.0

Earning 75 percent of college expenses.

Work Experience

- Glass Public Relations Company, Columbus, Ohio, Intern   6/XX to present

Assist with drafting copy for, designing, and proofreading public relations materials such as ad campaigns, brochures, and annual reports; use computer graphics programming, including Harvard Graphics.

- Lincoln University Trumpet, Columbus, Ohio, Student Reporter   9/XX to 6/XX

Wrote humor column on students' perspectives of campus life. Covered various academic departments; interviewed faculty from Humanities department on a regular basis; attended student organization meetings, and wrote summaries of student activities.

- Hewlett Bookstore, Suncity, Ohio, Assistant to Manager   6/XX to 9/XX

Responsible for stocking inventory for large bookstore; refined system for ordering and shelving stock; worked with promotional material; supervised three part-time workers.

Activities

Elected president of Alpha Kappa Phi business honorary; served on Dean's student advisory council, School of Business; member, National Business Students Association; co-chaired annual campuswide career fair.

Additional Skills

Computer skills   familiar with Vocus, Lotus, Cobol, Macintosh, Harvard Graphics
Languages   fluent in French

References

References are attached.

FIGURE 7.3   Chronological résumé #1.

DENNIS DOE

30 Raspberry Road
Columbus, Ohio 43213

614-924-3456
doe.9@liv.edu

PROFESSIONAL OBJECTIVE

To obtain a position as an account executive in the public relations field

KEY WORD SUMMARY

Leadership, internship, Web marketing

EDUCATION

Bachelor of Science, Business Administration, Lincoln University, Columbus, Ohio

Expected, June 2003

Major in marketing, minor in English; extensive coursework in consumer behavior, economics, technical writing, computer science, GPA 3.2/4.0

Earned 75 percent of college expenses.

SKILLS

Writing

- Assisted with drafting copy and proofreading of public relations materials during internship with Glass Public Relations Company.
- Reporter for student newspaper; wrote articles about academic departments and student organizations.
- Wrote weekly humor column on students' perspectives on campus life for college newspaper.

Organizational

- Organized campuswide Career Day; contacted over 100 employers to participate; arranged special work-shops as part of overall program.
- Responsible for stocking inventory for Hewlett Bookstore.
- Refined system for ordering and shelving stock.
- Supervised staff of three part-time workers.
- Worked with promotional material under manager's supervision.

Leadership

- Elected president of business honorary; acted as liaison with alumni in many types of businesses.
- Coordinated activities of 10-member committee for campuswide Career Day.
- Served on Dean's student advisory council.

EMPLOYMENT HISTORY

Glass Public Relations Company, Columbus, Ohio
June 2XXX to present
Hewlett Bookstore, Suncity, Ohio
June 2XXX to September 2XXX

ADDITIONAL SKILLS

- Computer skills—familiar with Vocus, Lotus, Cobol, Macintosh, Harvard Graphics, Microsoft Office
- Languages—fluent in French

FIGURE 7.4 Functional résumé.

MARLENE BROOK

current address: *permanent address:*
444 Stone Place   M.brook@college.net
Sheetrock, CA 93076   714-555-1898

OBJECTIVE   To obtain a position in an international company where I can use my proven sales
                      skills and fluency in French

EDUCATION   Sheetrock College, Sheetrock, CA
                      Bachelor of Arts, History major, French minor
                      May 2XXX, GPA 3.35

**PROFESSIONAL
EXPERIENCE**

6/XX–present   Third National Bank, Sheetrock, CA
                      Accounts Receivable Clerk

                      • Post deposit transactions
                      • Work with automated account system

6/XX–6/XX   Packard's Restaurant, Bryant, CA
                      Assistant Manager

                      • Responsible for operations of family restaurant's morning shift
                      • Directed work of four employees
                      • Increased sales through vigorous advertising campaign
                      • Started as waitress

6/XX–6/XX   Missus Clothes Horse, Bryant, CA
                      Salesperson

                      • Sold women's clothing in specialty shop
                      • Exceeded sales quota by 50 percent

ACTIVITIES   International Students Organization:
                      Volunteer mentor; assisted with orientation for new international students;
                      Union Board; created and coordinated student artwork program

ADDITIONAL   Computer training in, Microsoft Office, Macintosh

INFORMATION   Study Abroad Program: studied in Paris junior year of high school;
                      extensive travel in Europe; fluent in French
                      Earned 100 percent of college expenses

REFERENCES   Available upon request.

FIGURE 7.5 Chronological résumé #2.

MARY L. JONESFIELD

53 Oak Street, Apt. 203, Newport, Louisiana 70790   (232) 777-1234   M.Jonesfield@netlink.com

OBJECTIVE	To obtain an entry-level management position in retailing
SKILLS	• Experience in retail sales • Assisted in buying merchandise • Arranged floor displays • Resolved customer problems • Organized and maintained inventories
EDUCATION	B.A. in Communications, June 2XXX Cranston College, Evans, Louisiana Coursework emphasized organizational communications Courses in marketing, management, and consumer behavior
HONORS	Dean's List; Academic Scholarship
ACTIVITIES	Residence Hall Assistant; Elected representative to Undergraduate Student Government (two terms); President of Spanish Club
WORK EXPERIENCE *June 2XXX to present*	Gordon's Department Store, Bland, Louisiana *Salesperson* • Sell clothing in children's department • Learned extensive inventory • Developed sales techniques • Increased sales by 25 percent in six months
August 2XXX to July 2XXX	R. J. Imports, Newport, Louisiana *Salesperson* • Sold a variety of imported products, including bric-a-brac and clothing • Monitored and organized current stock • Started as stock person; promoted to sales after three months
ADDITIONAL INFORMATION	Competent in word processing, especially Microsoft Word Willing to travel or relocate

FIGURE 7.6 Skills résumé.

Steven R. Gall

Box 104, Appleton Hall, Conrad College, Micro, TN 38456   gall.42@aol.com   (595) 556-9876

JOB OBJECTIVE	To obtain an internship or summer employment in an art gallery or museum that will allow me to use my experience in art and my education in art history.
EDUCATION	Conrad College, 2XXX to present Bachelor of Arts, expected 2XXX GPA 3.0/4.0, Art History Major

WORK EXPERIENCE

Volunteer, Sojourn Museum   *Summer 2XXX*
Sojourn, TN
• Assisted in preparing three exhibits on contemporary art

Camp Counselor, Art Appreciation Camp   *Summer 2XXX*
Sunset, TN
• Counselor for children ages 7–10
• Developed and led printing and sculping art programs for small groups of children
• Assisted with waterfront activities

Volunteer, Francisco Gallery   *6/XX to 6/XX*
Sojourn, TN
• Helped arrange exhibits
• Served as docent for special showings with different customers including children and seniors
• Unpacked and prepared art materials for shipping

EXTRACURRICULAR
ACTIVITIES
• Theatre club-set designer
• Conrad college choir
• Arts council–elected student member
• Intramural volleyball

FIGURE 7.7 Summer job résumé.

WRITING A COVER LETTER

Along with your résumé, you should include a cover letter addressed to the specific person you want to contact. If you are not sure of the person to whom it should be sent, call the company for the appropriate contact. Ask for the correct spelling of the name and the person's title and address. A cover letter should be brief, but you may want to include additional information not on your résumé and emphasize experience specific to the job for which you are applying.

In the first paragraph, briefly indicate how you learned of the position and why you are interested in it. If you are responding to a job posting or ad, state the position title, where you saw the posting, and the date it was posted. If you were referred by an individual, state his or her name and title. In two or three additional paragraphs, review your relevant strengths and qualifications as they relate to this specific position. Do not repeat everything already included in your résumé; cover letters should be brief and to the point.

In a closing paragraph, indicate that you are available for an interview at the addressee's convenience. Always include a current phone number or e-mail address where you can be reached. (It is helpful to have a voice mail greeting that has a professional outgoing message so a prospective employer can leave a message if you do not answer.)

Your cover letter may be the hook that gets someone to read your résumé. Figures 7.8, 7.9, 7.10, and 7.11 are examples of cover letters. If you do not receive a response within two weeks of sending your résumé and cover letter, telephone the person to verify that it was received and inquire about your status.

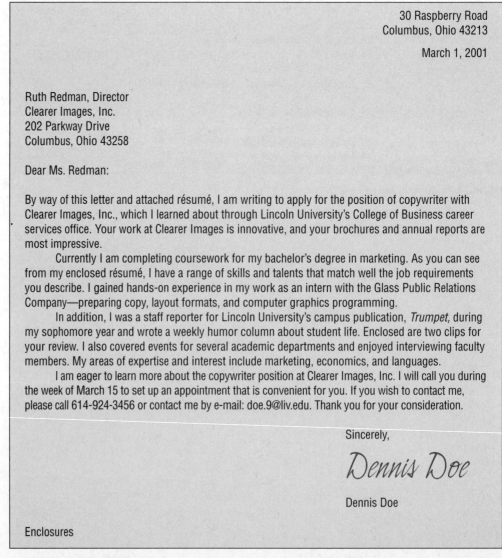

FIGURE 7.8   Cover letter #1.

2220 Smith Hall
18 S. 11th Avenue
Columbus, Ohio 43210

May 3, 2002

Al Jones
Director of Human Resources
Blank Management Systems
88 Stretch Drive
Cleveland, Ohio 40404

Dear Mr. Jones:

In response to the job posting for an accountant, which I reviewed at The Ohio State's College of Business career services office, I am enclosing my résumé. As you can see, I have worked in a variety of business settings and was fortunate to have been selected for a summer management-training internship at Acme, Inc. in 2XXX. In addition, my accounting degree has prepared me well for the specific tasks outlined in your job description, and I believe I would make a positive contribution to your company.

Being from the Cleveland area, I am familiar with your company's fine reputation and I am aware of the emphasis your firm places on strong managers and on hiring people with leadership skills. I would like to discuss with you in person what I can contribute to Blank Management Systems. Next week I will be in Cleveland and will telephone you to see if we can schedule an appointment to discuss my qualifications. I can be reached at denny.323@osu.edu or (614) 292-0000. Thank you for your consideration.

Sincerely,

Jane Denny

Jane Denny

Enclosure

FIGURE 7.9   Cover letter #2.

Cover letters sent by e-mail should be shorter and more to the point than mailed letters. They should fit in the browser window of your e-mail program (see Figure 7.11). You should be acquiring information and skills throughout your college years. Learning to write a résumé is one of the most basic skills in this process. First-year students benefit from seeing themselves on paper; it helps set goals, ascertain weaknesses, and use time and opportunities in college to acquire skills and experiences vital to becoming a strong job candidate. Upper-level students can convey to a prospective employer how they will appear on paper. As you continually update your résumé, include the positive changes and experiences you have gained that not only will enhance your perspective of your marketability but also will put you ahead of the game when it's time to find a job.

We have seen how you can reflect a positive, confident attitude through a well-organized résumé and a good cover letter. Preparing for the job search also requires skills to learn how to make direct contact with prospective employers. Chapter Eight discusses this important phase of the job-search process.

113 South Street
Appa, Idaho 35789

April 20, 2XXX

Mr. Alexander Q. Paul, Curator
Appa Museum of History
210 High Street
Appa, Idaho

Dear Mr. Ross:

Through this letter and attached résumé, I am applying for a position of museum educator with the Appa Museum of History. I will receive a bachelor's degree in history and anthropology from Springfield College in June. The excellent education I received in these areas is supported by hands-on work I have done in several museums. My knowledge, experience, and enthusiasm would be an asset to your enterprise.

As my résumé indicates, I have worked in museums both as an employee and a volunteer. I have assisted curators with research, set up exhibits, prepared objects for shipment, and acted as tour guide for many types of groups, including groups of children and senior citizens. At the Museum of History in Boise, I helped create exhibits about Western American Indian tribes that displayed many priceless artifacts.

Perhaps my most challenging experience was to participate in a dig with Professor Don Jones in southern Idaho, where American Indian artifacts have been discovered. Working on this dig allowed me to put my knowledge of history and anthropology to practical use and gave me a sense of the natural settings in which such artifacts should be displayed.

I look forward to talking with you in detail about how my education and work experience would be an asset to the Appa Museum of History. I will call you next week to request an appointment. In the meantime, I can be reached at Ott.7152@net.com or at 315-333-4040. Thank you for your consideration.

Sincerely,

Frederick Ott

Frederick Ott

Enclosure

FIGURE 7.10 Cover letter #3.

Subject: Candidate for museum educator position

Dear Mr. Ross:

I am applying for the position of Museum Educator at the Appa Museum of Art. As you can see from my attached résumé, I have many of the qualifications and experiences the position requires. I will graduate cum laude from Springfield College in June with a B.A. in history and a minor in anthropology. I have solid experience in developing and implementing programs for diverse audiences, including website programs. In my last internship with the Far Hills Museum, I developed learning materials for different grade levels and led tours of the museum's varied collection. I also assisted in training docents. I have worked part-time or volunteered in several other history museums during my college years and have gained a broad base of knowledge and skills. I know you will find me a motivated, resourceful individual and a hard working member of your team. Please let me know when I can set up an appointment to discuss my qualifications with you further.

Frederick Ott
Ott.7152@springfield.edu
777-643-8787

FIGURE 7.11   E-mail Cover Letter.

CASE STUDIES

Preparing

JED

As Jed checked the items in Chapter Seven on what he should be doing as a first-year student, he realized that he needed to be working on all of them, especially those related to academic work. To start taking some action toward his goal of teaching, he decided to apply for a summer job at his home city's recreation department to gain experience in that area. To do this, he had to write a résumé and learn how to interview. He used the résumé computer program in the campus' career services office and showed a rough draft to his career course instructor. His teacher offered some changes and additions and suggested that Jed show the next draft to an expert in the career services office. After a few more changes suggested by the résumé expert, Jed was confident that he had created a clear and concise picture of his skills and experiences for the recreation job.

At Christmas break Jed filled out an application and left his résumé and a cover letter with the recreation department. As a back-up, he applied at the swimming pool where he had been a lifeguard the previous two summers. He decided that at spring break he would apply for a summer sales job at a sporting goods store near his home. So he started researching the company's Web site. He also decided to volunteer as a baseball coach for a Little League team. Now that he had a direction and goal, he felt very good about the decisions he was making to carry out those goals.

MARIA

Maria had put together a résumé many years ago when she entered her first job out of high school, but she has updated it only sporadically. When she compared her résumé worksheet to those of some of the other students in the class, she realized that she had many skills and work experiences that the younger students did not. She realized that the computer skills she has been developing over the years are substantial and should be emphasized on her résumé.

An older student in the class told Maria about the help he had received from a counselor in the career services office on her campus, and Maria decided to take her final version there for a professional opinion. Although Maria is not job-hunting at this time, it occurs to her that she may be able to find a better paying position in another company to alleviate her financial situation. She plans to discuss with her present supervisor a possible promotion within the company. This will give her the motivation to update her résumé to reflect her new abilities and goals. ■

Summary Checklist

WHAT I HAVE LEARNED

____ I have learned the basic components of an effective résumé and gathered relevant information about myself in each of these areas.

____ I have written a résumé emphasizing my strengths and, through its appearance and format, portraying me in the best possible light.

____ I now recognize areas of my résumé that are weak and have established a plan to acquire the skills and experiences needed to make me an outstanding job candidate.

____ I have the skills to submit an electronic résumé and can identify and use job-search Web sites on the Internet.

____ I understand the importance of a cover letter, its purpose, and what it should include.

HOW I CAN USE IT

I can write an impressive résumé and feel confident that an employer will want to interview me after reading it.

CHAPTER 8

Am I the Best Candidate?
Job Leads and the Job Interview

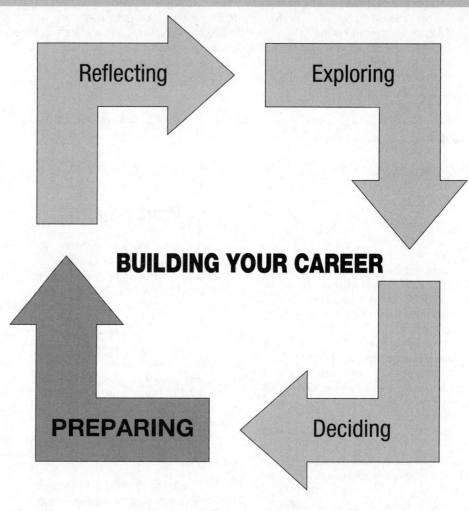

The closest a person ever comes to perfection is when he fills out a job application form.

STANLEY J. RANDELL

GENERATING JOB LEADS

In the preceding chapters you reviewed and refined your personal perspectives of "career," examined your personal characteristics and how they might be compatible with certain career fields, experienced the decision-making process, and learned about the future work world. In addition, you learned how to present yourself in the best possible light using different types of résumés. The next step is to present yourself to a prospective employer as an applicant for a specific job. If you already hold a job or have worked part-time, you probably have been interviewed. This chapter provides information about the interviewing process and its part in ensuring a successful outcome.

One of the most important sources of job openings is the "hidden market." According to the U.S. Department of Labor, 80% of all positions are filled without employer advertising and are often filled by candidates referred by recommendations from in-house employees, recruiters, or direct contact with candidates. Employers are looking for suitable candidates to replace departing, returning, or ineffective workers or to staff new projects. Although the Internet has changed dramatically how many job seekers search and apply for jobs, networking and other methods are key to finding jobs in the hidden job market. The job hunting resource descriptions discussed next will help you formulate a plan for generating contacts. Suggestions for job searching on the Internet follow these more traditional sources.

Job Search Sources

NETWORKING   Networking might be the most important resource for obtaining job leads. Creating a network of people to contact in your job search is critical. You can build your network by talking with friends, family, faculty members, and past employers. Other sources include contacts made through student organizations, alumni databases, or on-campus interviews arranged by your career services office. If you ask every individual you talk with for one or two possible "leads," in time your networking efforts likely will lead to an actual job interview. Be sure to record carefully in a computer file or notebook the name of any referral, as well as his or her title, e-mail address, phone number, and address, and who referred you to that individual.

As previously noted, careful preparation is essential before actually making contact. Be certain you are clear about why this person's job is relevant to your own job search before asking for an appointment. Networking letters to people you know or have been referred to can be more informal than a regular cover letter since you are not asking for a job but for time and expertise. Figure 8.1 is an example of a networking contact letter.

NEWSPAPERS   Newspapers are still a valuable tool for finding job leads at the local level. Reading the classified ads section is one way to keep abreast of the market. Again, newspapers do not list most jobs, but they can be another resource to consider. Following up on a newspaper ad can provide the type of experience you need to sharpen your cover letters and, sometimes, your interviewing skills.

EMPLOYMENT SERVICES   Entry-level jobs occasionally are listed with employment agencies, which receive a commission on every position they fill. Interviewing for a job through an employment service is good practice for determining the effectiveness of your résumé and interviewing skills. Experienced workers may want to contact a "headhunter," a person who works for an employment service to place people in high-level positions.

If you are required to sign an agreement with an employment service, be certain that you understand the terms of the contract. Sometimes the employer pays the commission. Other contracts require the employee to pay a fee. Companies that specialize in temporary employment assignments could provide opportunities to launch your career.

Subject: Referral from Dr. Ian Higgins

Dear Ms. Oxley:

Dr. Ian Higgins at Tower College referred me to you for information about the field of dietetics. I will graduate in June with a B.S. in Dietetics and am interested in seeking a job in the field after graduation. I am currently an intern at Hope Hospital as part of my training, and the experience has solidified my desire to pursue this career area.

Would you be willing to spare a brief amount of time to give me your perspective on the field of dietetics? I will call you Thursday of next week (October 7) to see if you are willing to see me. I can be reached at stilt@dotnet.net or 611-299-7788. Thank you for your consideration.

Jonus Stilt

FIGURE 8.1 E-mail Networking Contact Letter.

JOB FAIRS Your school may offer a job fair, so which prospective employers are invited to share information about their company or services with students in a large, informal setting. Students have the opportunity to peruse different companies by walking from table to table, picking up printed information, and talking personally with company representatives who can explain the type of work they do, the jobs they have opened, and the background, training, and personal attributes they seek in prospective employees. To manage a job fair successfully, students should have realistic expectations (i.e., this is an opportunity to network, not to "get a job"); they should follow up with employers they meet.

Job fairs are excellent vehicles for gathering information and asking questions in an informal setting. Even though you may be only a first- or second-year student, you can learn a great deal by attending job fairs. As an upper-level student, you can easily and quickly expand your contacts and learn about new employment possibilities.

FRIENDS AND FAMILY Many people find jobs through personal contacts gleaned from family, friends, or acquaintances. Other possibilities are friends of friends, parents of friends, and acquaintances. These leads are fruitful because the employer is more apt to view you positively on the basis of a good recommendation from a mutual contact than from a "cold call" or "blind résumé." When using this type of referral, your goal is to get an interview. When you do, it is up to you to make a strong case for why you are the best person for the job.

DIRECT CONTACTS Targeting specific types of employers can be a productive approach. You can study the type of work they perform and determine if it matches your own interests and skills. Send a résumé with a cover letter to a *specific individual,* indicating why you would like to meet with that person. Then follow up with a phone call. Often your résumé will be prescreened, so the employer may not see it. Be persistent in your effort. When you finally reach the person, be prepared to impress the individual with your knowledge of the company and how your background, training, and experience would make you an asset to the organization. The idea here is to persuade the potential employer to meet with you. Use the suggestions in the "interviewing" section of Chapter Three whenever you make personal contacts.

Although people are busy, they often enjoy discussing their job with students or others who are in the process of exploring career possibilities. Share the information you have already obtained about their field from your research, and ask if it is accurate from their perspective. You also may want to ask your interviewees for names of other people in similar positions so you may *extend your interviewing network.*

Stick to the time you have allotted. Thank the interviewees for their insights and follow up with a thank-you letter. Keep a spreadsheet that includes interviewee's name, title, place of employment, and the important facts you obtained. Other job search sources are student organizations, Alumni Databases, Job posting Web sites and on-campus interviews.

CAREER MENTORS

Many successful workers have been helped by someone who has given them guidance—a mentor who helped them learn important things about their work environment and career. A mentor is an experienced person who has "been there" and is willing to help a new associate. Mentors can give advice and personal support. They can help you develop knowledge and skills that are essential for you to become integrated into a new work environment and better understand what the job requires. You may already have a mentor in another part of your life (e.g., school, community activity). That person also may be an excellent source of information for possible networking contacts or even job prospects.

JOB SEARCHING ON THE INTERNET

Job searching on the Internet can be difficult and time-consuming since it requires accessing many different sources. The vast array of networks, job lead banks, lists, and other formats can be overwhelming. To focus your search, decide what specific occupational fields interest you. What do you want to do in your job? What type of company, industry, or organization do you want to work for? The U.S. government Web site O*Net, which you used in Chapters Two and

Three is a good place to start. The career sections of company Web sites are another excellent source of specific information.

Examples of other sites that provide sources of employment and career information services, including tips for résumé writing include the following:

- www.rileyguide.com
- www.careerbuilder.com
- www.vault.com
- www.monster.com
- www.quintcareers.com

Don't make the mistake, however, of just looking for jobs on the Internet. Most of your search time should be spent on contacts with people who can give you job leads and referrals as well as suggestions and advice. The Internet can give you information to enlarge your search and can help you generate focused questions.

JOB INTERVIEWING

The purpose of a job interview is to offer the opportunity for an employer to know what sets you apart from other candidates. Although your résumé lists your work experiences, educational background, and skills, during the interview you can elaborate on this information while impressing upon the interviewer what you can bring to the position. A thorough preparation before the interview is critical to making the best possible impression.

If you previously interviewed people about occupations that interest you (Chapter Three) or academic majors you are considering (Chapter Four), you probably have a wealth of valuable information that can help you now. Interviewing workers in their place of work can help you gain insights into the person's daily tasks, background and experience, personal reflections on the work, information about promotions and other opportunities for advancement, how the career choice has affected the person's lifestyle, and recommended preparations.

It is helpful to think of interviewing in three stages: *preparing* for the interview, how to conduct yourself *during* the interview, and what to do *after* the interview. When direct contact, résumés, and cover letters result in an interview, how you prepare is vital. Most screening interviews last about 30 minutes, and the first 5 minutes usually set the tone. First impressions are important.

Preparing for the Interview

The importance of researching the business or organization before the interview cannot be emphasized enough. Thorough research will tell you if the company or organization is of interest to you and if you are a good fit. As you research each company or organization, keep a record of important information as you gather it. The following are a few examples of basic questions to research:

- What does the company do (services and/or products)?
- How is the company organized (primary business units)? Where is the company located (headquarters, branch offices, international offices, retail outlets, etc.)?
- What kind of training programs does the company provide?
- What kind of career paths exist in your field?
- What are the salary ranges or hourly rates paid for various positions?
- What is the company's track record with recent graduates (retention, turnover, etc.)?
- What are some titles of positions that interest you?
- How does this organization fit your specific career plans and goals?

In addition to the Internet and the company's literature, talk to professionals in the field, students, and recent graduates for additional information.

Any information you have learned about the company and other prospective places of employment will tell the interviewees you are serious about working there. Most companies publish information about their purpose, priorities, and financial situation, as well as other pertinent facts on their Web site. You also can obtain this information from annual reports, product information brochures, library resources, business databases services and newspapers. This type of information also is available at your career office or directly from the company. Studying the information can help you prepare relevant questions, focus on employers' needs, and understand how you can contribute to their mission. Anxiety about interviews is natural, but you will be more relaxed and confident if you feel well-prepared.

Many career services offices offer workshops on how to interview. Some even provide the opportunity for you to do a mock interview with a professional employer, who then gives feedback on your performance. Or you can organize mock interviews with your friends and family. Practice builds interviewing skills and teaches you habits to avoid, such as not making eye contact and talking too much. If you are able to arrange a mock interview with an employer, ask questions to elicit feedback, such as the following:

What was your first impression of me?

What was your impression of my overall appearance? Physical and nonverbal mannerisms? Tone and speed of speech?

How would you rate my listening skills?

How clear was I in expressing my personal goals and objectives?

How would you rate the discussion of my educational and work experiences?

What was my level of knowledge of the organization and the position I was applying for?

How did I respond to the substance of your questions?

Did I ask relevant and thoughtful questions as the interview progressed?

What was your impression of my level of enthusiasm and interest in the position?

Would you hire me? Why or why not?

During the Interview

You want to convey an image of confidence throughout the interview. If you have prepared carefully, you probably will relax once it is under way and realize you are able to ask and answer questions succinctly and comfortably. Try to analyze the interviewer's style, and respond in the same manner. Behave formally if the interviewer sets a formal tone. If the interviewer asks questions quickly and moves on to the next, respond similarly.

Interviewers are quick to pick up on nonverbal mannerisms that indicate nervousness (e.g., looking around the room, nervously fingering your pen). Make good eye contact, listen intently, and ask and answer questions thoughtfully. Be well-prepared, but don't practice so much that you sound "canned." Be spontaneous and honest. An honest self-evaluation will impress an interviewer. Be prepared to talk about your strengths as well as your weaknesses. You can turn a shortcoming into a positive statement:

"One of my weaknesses is being a perfectionist. I'm a diligent worker, but I'm getting better at understanding that everything doesn't have to be perfect."

Interviewers often ask similar basic questions. Anticipating these questions gives you a chance to formulate your answers and practice them in mock interview sessions. Other questions may depend on the type of position or the interviewer's style. Sample questions an interviewer might ask include:

Tell me about yourself.

Why are you applying for this position?

Do you understand what this job entails? (A discussion of the job can lead to observations about your abilities, experiences, attitudes, etc.)

What are your greatest strengths? What are your greatest weaknesses?

Can you give me an example of a leadership role you have played?

Give me an example of adversity you have faced and how you overcame it.

Name two or three accomplishments that have given you the most satisfaction.

How did you finance your college education? What does your grade point tell me about you?

Do you have any other information about yourself that would help me make a decision about filling this job?

One frequently asked question is, "Tell me about yourself." You might respond briefly by describing the personal qualities that are relevant to the position for which you are interviewing. Describe your educational background, related work experience, and some of your personal strengths. For example:

> "I will graduate in June with a degree in communications. I was president of the communications club and was elected to our college's administrative council. I interned twice with a local public relations firm and was invited to work part-time as a result of that experience. I'm a hard worker and well organized. I'm an excellent writer and have been told I have creative ways of approaching different problems."

Another common question is, "Why do you want this job?" This is a good time to reiterate your goals, strengths, special qualities, and how they relate to the job for which you are interviewing.

> "My goal is to obtain a position where I can use my interests and talents in writing and marketing. Your position is very appealing because it appears to offer the type of work I love and have prepared for. My internship experiences confirmed my interest in public relations, and I think I can contribute a great deal to your organization."

Although you should wait for the interviewer to bring up the question of salary, you should be prepared for the question, "What salary do you expect?" You will already have studied the salary range for the job for which you are applying—or a specific salary may have been designated for the job. Your career services office should have salary data that you can use. Your knowledge about the salary will show the interviewer you have done your homework. If you are not certain, ask for more details before responding.

Employers sometimes are more influenced by negative information than positive information. Even though you are presenting yourself in your most favorable light, your interviewers often give more weight to unfavorable information or impressions to narrow down the field. Even a small negative may shift an interviewer's impression—for example, saying you are never available to work overtime.

You also should be prepared to ask questions of your own based on the information you have gathered. Writing them down ahead of time will help you organize your thoughts. You might ask your interviewer about other students from your school who are employed by the company and how they have advanced. Listen for value-laden statements by the interviewer, such as those concerning expectations about work-time commitment. Ask questions about the company policies that are important to you. Try to determine if your work values match those of the company's culture. As you research the company, write down questions you want to ask in the interview.

INTERVIEW FORMATS Employers may use one of several types of interview formats, including the traditional question-and-answer session, in which an interviewer and interviewee use a *structured* format. The *unstructured* style is similar to a conversation. A more recent type is the *targeted* or behavioral interviewing approach, in which the questions asked are used to measure the interviewee's potential in critical areas such as problem solving and leadership. The interviewee is asked to cite examples of past performance in designated areas.

A strategy for helping you effectively respond to behavioral based questions is the STAR Technique. STAR stands for situation, tasks, actions, and results. Interviewees are asked about a time they used a specific skill or exhibited a specific quality. When responding they should describe the major *tasks* in that situation, the *actions* they took and the *results* (outcomes). Examples of target questions might be: "Describe a situation where you had to talk to an individual or group causing a problem" or "Tell me about the most difficult decision you've ever had to make." Your answers should be based on actual past or current situations. Your focus should be on reporting factual information, not hypothetical situations. Responses to these types of questions require preparation, so think through (*before* the interview) possible situations that include all the components of a complete STAR.

Types of interviews. In addition to the traditional one-on-one interview, you may also encounter a group interview where several candidates are interviewed simultaneously. You may also experience a panel interview where several people will be asking you questions. Make sure you understand the dynamics of these interview settings and prepare accordingly. The professionals in your career services office can give you pointers on how to prepare for different types of interview settings.

CYBER-INTERVIEWS   Software is now available for interviewing job applicants. Prospective employees are asked a series of questions about their career goals and work history. Applicants' responses are rated, and those with the highest ratings are invited for a personal interview.

APPEARANCE   Making a good impression includes physical appearance as well as how you ask and respond to questions. How you dress sometimes depends on the type of job you are seeking. In some fields (such as business or engineering), professional dress (suit) is expected for all interviews. Other fields, such as teaching or social work, may be less formal and may allow business casual dress. When you present an attractive appearance, the interviewer will know you are aware of the importance of conveying a professional image. Find out how people dress in the work environment where you are interviewing. A safe approach is to wear conservative, contemporary, but comfortable clothes for any interview, even if the employees are allowed to wear jeans. Use jewelry and fragrance in moderation. In any event, an interviewer often will measure your seriousness and maturity by your appearance.

ETIQUETTE   Although old-fashioned manners often are taken for granted, some job seekers need a refresher course. It is always proper for men and women alike to stand to shake hands when being greeted, for example. Table manners at a business lunch can communicate volumes about a candidate. In the Internet age, etiquette in the job-search process is changing constantly. When in doubt, use common sense. A traditional approach is probably best when no clear rule exists.

After the Interview

You should write a follow-up thank-you letter or e-mail to the interviewer to reiterate your interest in the position. A phone call also might be valuable. Reflect on the interview and write down areas in which you did well and those in which you need to improve. Be realistic in your evaluation of the outcomes of the interview.

Keep a running account of the date and place of all interviews and names, titles, and other important information about the interviewers. After the interviews, immediately write down your impressions of what was discussed. Record pertinent e-mail addresses, phone numbers, follow-up, and other information. Keep a careful record of every contact, as you may forget important details needed later.

Follow-up letters leave a favorable impression and can make a critical difference. In some cases, they can help you stand out if you had a successful interview. Include a brief note of appreciation plus a reminder of your special skills or qualities.

If you are invited for a second interview, continue to use the same approaches you have employed successfully to date. Another visit to the company will help you confirm your feeling about how good a fit the organization is for you as well as for them.

EXERCISE 8.1   Interview Follow-Up

After an interview, record your answers to the following questions:

How has this compared to your past experience with job interviews?

_____

_____

_____

_____

What part of the job interview process do you need to work on the most? Why?

_____

_____

_____

What specific steps can you take now to prepare for future interview situations?

_____

_____

_____

_____

_____

LEGAL AND ILLEGAL INQUIRIES

The Fair Employment Practices Act designates certain hiring practices as illegal. These include procedures and questions related to interviewing. Employers are not allowed to inquire about nationality, religious affiliation, age, race, marital status, pregnancy, disabilities, arrest records, or drug or alcohol addiction. If you think this information is relevant to the position, however, you can volunteer the information.

If you think you have been asked an illegal question, you may want to answer it with another question (e.g., "In what way is this related to this position?"). Or if the question is an obvious violation, you need to be assertive and give your reason for not answering. Violations should be reported to the director of your campus career services office if the interview took place under its auspices, so appropriate action may be taken. _How_ questions are asked is also important.

Information may vary slightly depending on differences in state and local laws. The following are a few examples of illegal interview questions:

- How tall are you?
- How much do you weigh?
- Are you married?
- Will you need any special accommodations to do your job?
- Were you born in the United States?
- How old are you?
- Do you belong to a union?
- What are the name and address of your nearest relative to be notified in case of an emergency?

The U.S. Department of Labor's Web site (www.dol.gov) is the most reliable source for information about worker rights.

Other illegal questions are those pertaining to race, color, past or current medical conditions not related to the specific job, your religious preferences, willingness to work on religious holidays, and disabilities. Other _legal_ questions include inquiries into applicants' experience in organizations that is relevant to their potential job performance; inquiries about references (for example, "Who suggested that you apply for this position?" or asking for names of persons willing to provide proof and/or character references); inquiries about place and duration of residence; inquiries into applicants' academic, vocational, or professional education and schools attended; and inquiries into work experiences.

To summarize, interviewers are generally looking for certain attributes in an interviewee—namely, maturity, enthusiasm, creativity, and confidence, as well as thoughtfulness and intelligence. Do not underestimate the importance of careful preparation. Practicing your interviewing techniques in many situations can give you the experience you will need for your "dream job" interview. You want to make the most favorable impression possible. Be spontaneous, and direct and present your best self.

DEALING WITH REJECTION

In spite of your careful preparation and planning, you may not find a job right away. In normal times, the average job search can take from six months to a year. This can be a discouraging experience, and you may start to put yourself down or feel inadequate. If this happens, take positive steps. Review your job-search approach and determine areas for improvement (e.g., résumé, how you make contacts, interviewing). Ask yourself these questions:

Am I willing to take a lower-level position with the possibility of using it as a stepping-stone to a better one? (You risk selling yourself short, so be aware of future opportunities with the company rather than using it as an "out" for the present situation.)

Have I used all the resources available to me (e.g., untapped leads/referrals, alumni contacts)?

Do I have the resources to volunteer in a setting that would provide the experience I need?

Can I reach my career goal in other ways (e.g., shift my focus to another job area)?

Would further education enhance my prospects in my chosen career area?

Exercise 8.2 provides a means to record your thoughts about unsuccessful interviews.

EXERCISE 8.2   Handling Rejection

Answering the following questions may help you deal with rejection and plan some alternative strategies.

Have you ever been refused a job? If so, describe your reaction and what you would do differently *now* in that interview situation.

_____

_____

_____

If you have never been rejected from a job, how do you think you would react in that situation?

_____

_____

_____

JOB SEARCH REVIEW

Reexamining the requirements for future workers outlined in Chapters Three and Six may give you some clues for exploring personal qualifications and possible new occupational environments. Finding a job requires patience, fortitude, and self-confidence. You eventually will find a position if you persevere and take a proactive approach.

Learning how to organize and carry out a job search is a complicated endeavor best started during your freshman year in college, but it is never too late to initiate the critical tasks involved in the process. You must be constantly aware of the resources available to help you reach your goal.

The skills you develop in the job-search process will carry over into the work world once you are hired. Managing a job-search campaign can help you appreciate the value of being organized, learning to write succinctly, learning how to do research and solve problems, learning how to communicate in a variety of situations, and building confidence in your abilities. These are attributes that many employers seek in an employee.

The suggestions below summarize the primary job-search components discussed in the last two chapters:

1. Start preparing for your job search as early as possible. You must accomplish many tasks before your senior year.
2. Employers prefer to interview and hire academically capable students over academically marginal ones.
3. Be active in work-related and campus volunteer activities that can provide the type of experiences you can use later to sell yourself.
4. Establish a résumé file or worksheet on which you continue to record your goals, accomplishments, work experience, and other information during your college years.
5. If possible, take part in co-op or internship experiences to strengthen your work record in a given field.
6. Prepare for interviews by researching information about prospective employers.
7. Practice your interviewing techniques in as many settings as you can, and ask for feedback. Your confidence and skill level will increase with each experience.
8. Follow up each contact with a letter of appreciation.
9. Check your progress regularly regarding whether you are achieving your career goals.
10. Be enthusiastic about selling yourself and your unique qualities. You're worth it!

CASE STUDIES

Preparing

JED

To prepare for his interviews for a summer job, Jed went to several workshops offered by the career services office on his campus. He learned about the importance of preparing before the interview, because knowing as much as possible about the organization can help him answer and ask questions. Jed took advantage of the opportunity to videotape himself in a mock interview with a professional employer. As he talked, he was surprised to see the little habits that were distracting.

The employer complimented Jed on his poise and confidence but offered several good suggestions for improvement. Jed also practiced his interviewing techniques on several family members and friends to be as well prepared as possible for the real thing.

MARIA

When Maria went to her college's career services office to show her résumé to a career counselor, she signed up for a workshop on interviewing skills. As soon as she feels confident, she will make an appointment with her current supervisor to try what she has learned. After exploring the possibilities within her company, Maria will de-cide whether to start the job-search process in earnest.

A friend has told her about some jobs she is qualified for in another company that is offering much higher salaries than what Maria is currently making. Maria must weigh the financial difference between a better salary at another company against the benefit of free tuition from her present employer. Maria feels confident that her newly acquired job-search skills will give her an advantage if and when she decides to look for a new job. ▪

Summary Checklist

WHAT I HAVE LEARNED

_____ I know how to generate job leads using specific contacts and resources.

_____ I have contacted my career-planning office or other resources for help in perfecting my job-search skills and have signed up for workshops or other help in developing these skills.

_____ I feel confident I know how to conduct myself in a job-interviewing situation before, during, and after the contact and have practiced in a simulated or real setting.

HOW I CAN USE IT

I know the steps in mounting a job search that will lead to interviews with a prospective employer and feel confident of my ability to market myself in an interview situation.

CHAPTER 9

Where Do I Go from Here?

Throughout this book you have examined many facets of career exploration and planning:

- You have learned about work in general and how your own perceptions of work might influence your choices.
- You have learned a process for career decision making and have become familiar with the knowledge, skills, attitudes, and behaviors necessary to progress through the process.
- You have examined and evaluated your personal strengths, such as the skills, interests, values, and personality traits that make you a unique person.
- You have explored occupational areas and learned how to access and evaluate occupational information.
- You have identified educational options that lead to or complement possible occupational areas.
- You have glimpsed the workplace of the future and learned about the type of workers employers will be hiring.
- You have, perhaps, decided on a general or even a specific occupational or educational direction.

To help you determine where you are in the career decision-making process and where to go from here, consider the three methods in Exercises 9.1, 9.2, and 9.3. Exercise 9.1 will help you see where you are at this point in your career planning. As a further check on where you need to go from here and to help you pull together everything you have learned, examine the flowchart in Figure 9.1. It can help you assemble the pieces of the larger picture into a coherent whole through a step-by-step process. It also suggests resources. Exercise 9.2 invites you to use Figure 9.1 in evaluating your career path thus far. Exercise 9.3 asks you to fill out the checklist, then compare it to the one you completed in Exercise 1.6, Chapter One.

EXERCISE 9.1   Method 1

A Snapshot in the Career-Planning Process

Check where you are now in the career-planning process by revisiting the stages outlined in Chapter One, Figure 1.1.

I believe I am now in the _____ phase of the career decision-making process because

_____

_____

_____

_____

_____

EXERCISE 9.2   Method 2

Evaluating Your Career Planning

Referring to Figure 9.1, you will be able to trace your career journey to this point.

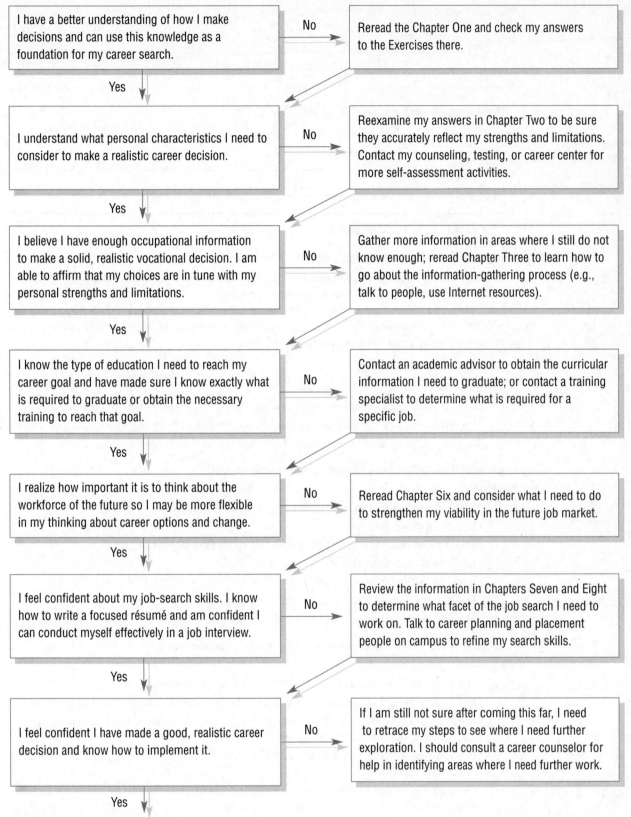

I have a better understanding of how I make decisions and can use this knowledge as a foundation for my career search.

No → Reread the Chapter One and check my answers to the Exercises there.

Yes ↓

I understand what personal characteristics I need to consider to make a realistic career decision.

No → Reexamine my answers in Chapter Two to be sure they accurately reflect my strengths and limitations. Contact my counseling, testing, or career center for more self-assessment activities.

Yes ↓

I believe I have enough occupational information to make a solid, realistic vocational decision. I am able to affirm that my choices are in tune with my personal strengths and limitations.

No → Gather more information in areas where I still do not know enough; reread Chapter Three to learn how to go about the information-gathering process (e.g., talk to people, use Internet resources).

Yes ↓

I know the type of education I need to reach my career goal and have made sure I know exactly what is required to graduate or obtain the necessary training to reach that goal.

No → Contact an academic advisor to obtain the curricular information I need to graduate; or contact a training specialist to determine what is required for a specific job.

Yes ↓

I realize how important it is to think about the workforce of the future so I may be more flexible in my thinking about career options and change.

No → Reread Chapter Six and consider what I need to do to strengthen my viability in the future job market.

Yes ↓

I feel confident about my job-search skills. I know how to write a focused résumé and am confident I can conduct myself effectively in a job interview.

No → Review the information in Chapters Seven and Eight to determine what facet of the job search I need to work on. Talk to career planning and placement people on campus to refine my search skills.

Yes ↓

I feel confident I have made a good, realistic career decision and know how to implement it.

No → If I am still not sure after coming this far, I need to retrace my steps to see where I need further exploration. I should consult a career counselor for help in identifying areas where I need further work.

Yes ↓

Congratulations! You are on your way.

FIGURE 9.1   Flowchart: A path to a career decision.

If you wish to retrace some steps, what are they?

_____
_____
_____
_____

What resources will you need in retracing these steps?

_____
_____
_____
_____
_____

EXERCISE 9.3 Method 3

My Career and Life-Planning Checklist Revisited

In Chapter One, Exercise 1.5, you checked the items in the following list that you wanted to learn about to make effective educational and career decisions.

   Now check the same items below based on *what you have actually learned* and compare your answers with those in Exercise 6.1. This should give you an idea of the tools you now have to continue your career exploration and planning.

Chapter One: Am I Ready?
I Know:

_____ what is involved in career and life planning and where I am currently in the process.

_____ I am ready to take the time and responsibility **now** to actively engage in career planning.

_____ how my perception of "work" might influence my career choices.

Chapter Two: What Do I Need to Know About Myself?
I Know:

_____ how my personality might influence my occupational choices.

_____ my occupational interests.

_____ what I value in a job (e.g., income, co-workers, self-employment).

_____ my current skills and what new ones I need to learn.

_____ how I can build on my strengths.

_____ how my family background might affect my career choices.

_____ how my gender might influence my career choices.

Chapter Three: How Do I Search for Occupational Information?
I Know:

_____ how to identify occupations that are realistic for me to explore.

_____ how I can compare my interests, values, and skills to certain occupational alternatives.

_____ where I can find important information about specific occupations (e.g., salaries, required skills, educational requirements, employment trends).

_____ the best sources for finding occupational information (e.g., Internet, printed, electronic, personal interviews).

_____ the experiences that will help me test my ideas about an occupational field (e.g., internships, volunteer work, study abroad).

_____ how to evaluate and use occupational information once I have found it.

Chapter Four: What Do I Need to Know About Educational Alternatives?
I Know:

_____ how certain majors match my personal academic strengths.

_____ where I can find information about specific majors (e.g., talk to faculty, academic advisors, seniors in major, alumni).

_____ the occupational fields that relate to the college major(s) I am considering/pursuing.

_____ the type of education I will need to enter certain occupational fields (e.g., two or four-year degree, technical degree, graduate or professional study).

_____ how I can identify the courses that will strengthen the knowledge and skills I will need for certain jobs.

Chapter Five: How Will I Decide?

I Know:

_____ why understanding my personal style of making decisions is important.

_____ how I can learn to become a more effective career decision maker.

_____ how I can be more effective and realistic in setting short- and long-term goals.

_____ how to put into action the educational and/or career decisions I have made.

_____ why reevaluating career decisions periodically is so important.

Chapter Six: How Can I Prepare for the Future Workplace?

I Know:

_____ the factors that are influencing the present and future workplace.

_____ the workforce and hiring trends for the next 5 to 10 years.

_____ how I can search for information about the job outlook for the occupational fields I am considering.

_____ the qualities that employers will value in the future workplace and how I can begin to make myself more marketable.

Chapter Seven: How Will I Advance My Career? The Job Search and Résumé Writing

I Know:

_____ the important job-search skills I need to learn.

_____ the important qualities of an effective résumé.

_____ the essentials in writing a good cover letter.

_____ how to use technology and other methods to search for a job.

Chapter Eight: Am I the Best Candidate? Job Leads and the Job Interview

I Know:

_____ how to generate job leads.

_____ the best way to prepare for a job interview.

_____ what good interview behavior entails.

_____ where I can learn about cyber-interviews and other electronic methods.

_____ what is important to do for an interview follow-up.

Chapter Nine: Where Do I Go from Here?

I Know:

_____ where I am now in the career decision-making process.

_____ what action steps I need to take next to continue my career planning.

Compare the items you checked on Exercise 1.6 with the same items you just checked. Have you accomplished what you intended?

_____ yes _____ no

If yes, you have made excellent progress. If no, what areas still need work?

_____

_____

_____

_____

_____

_____

As a final exercise, Exercise 9.4 is intended to help you formulate an action plan for the future.

EXERCISE 9.4   Action Planning

Below, write some short- and long-term career goals you wish to accomplish in the future.

Short-term goals (to be accomplished within the next school term or year):

_____

_____

_____

_____

_____

_____

_____

Long-term goals (to be accomplished in the next two or three years):

_____

_____

_____

_____

_____

_____

_____

Compare these goals with the ones you set in Chapter Five. Have you met any of your original goals? Are they still the same? Did you add any new ones?

Throughout this book we have emphasized that the career-planning process is a lifelong task. If you have made an educational and/or occupational decision at this point, congratulations!

If you have not yet decided, you now have an understanding of the knowledge, skills, attitudes, and behaviors needed to continue the search. By using the information and guidelines provided in this book, you can feel confident that you have the expertise to make personally satisfying career decisions now and in the future.

CASE STUDIES

Jed and Maria

JED

Although Jed has made a choice of major and a general career direction, he knows that these are tentative decisions. Because he is still in his first year, many factors must come into play before his tentative goals can be fulfilled. Jed must earn a certain gradepoint average to apply for the education program at his college, as it is selective. He has decided, therefore, to concentrate on his coursework and has vowed to discipline himself to follow certain study habits.

Jed has set a schedule for studying, while at the same time realizing the importance of recre-ation and being with friends. He knows it is impor-tant to reach a balance in his life while enjoying the college experience. This is a new feeling for Jed, who usually took things as they came with little planning or thought about the future. He is confident in his ability to be flexible and open to change and looks forward to the rest of his experience.

MARIA

Maria has just finished the last exercises in *Building Your Career.* She is pleased with what she has learned about herself and the computer job market. She has decided to pursue computer sci-ence as a major. She realizes that she must man-age her non-work schedule carefully to include class and study time. She believes she has sharp-ened her decision-making skills and knows how to prepare a strong résumé. Her action plan includes exploring new job possibilities within her present company and continuing to explore some specific skills she has identified that will be marketable in her current job or a new one. ■

CASE STUDY

Me

Making educational and career decisions is an important part of life. Throughout this book, you have progressed through a very personal journey. Although the decisions you have made so far are probably tentative, you have experienced a process that you will repeat many times in the future. Reflect on where you *were* when you started this journey, where you *are* now in making decisions, and where you *want* to be after graduation. For example: How are you feeling about your current decisions? How are you feeling about your college experience at this point? What you are looking forward to accomplishing in the next two or three years?

_____

_____

_____

_____

_____

_____

_____

_____

_____

_____

_____

_____

_____

REFERENCES

Gioia, J., & Herman, R. (2005, November–December). Career planning for the 21st century. *The Futurist*.

Holland, J. (1997). *Making Vocational Choices*. Odessa, FL: Psychological Assessment Resources.

Lombardo, T. (2006, January). *Thinking Ahead: The Value of Future Consciousness. The Futurist*.

Ludden, L., Shatkin, L., & Farr, J. M. (2001). *Guide for Occupational Exploration,* 3rd ed. St. Paul, MN: JIST Publishing.

Trilling, B., & Fadel, C. (2009). *21st Century Skills: Learning for Life in Our Times*. San Francisco: Jossey-Bass.

INDEX

Note: Page numbers followed by "f" indicate figures; followed by "t" indicate table

A

Abilities. *See also* Skills
  defined, 16
Action steps, in job search, 78–79
Action verbs, used for résumé, 84, 85
Alternative solutions, for decision making
  choosing, 64–65
  listing, 63–64
America's Career InfoNet, 31
America's Service Locator, 31
Appearance, in job interview, 104
Artistic (creator) personality type, 11
Artistic interests, 14t
  and associated skills, 19t
  and work values, 16t
Assessment
  of interests, 12–14
  of work values, 15, 16

B

Baby-boomer generation, workforce and, 70
Baccalaureate degree, 38, 41
Barriers, to career choice, 4–5
  overcoming, 5
Behavioral interviewing approach, 103
Bureau of Labor Statistics. *See* U.S. Bureau of Labor Statistics
Business, as occupation, 72

C

Career
  building, 6f
  development process, 2
  flowchart, 109f
  and life skills, 74–75
  theorists on, 1
Career and Life Planning Checklist, 7–8
Career choice
  action plan, 65–66
  alternatives and, 63–65
  barriers to, 4–5
  environmental factors and, 20–24
  family and, 20–22
  gender and, 23
  overcoming barriers to, 5
  personality and, 11
  process, 6
  review, 66–67
  socioeconomic status (SES) and, 20
Career genogram, 20–23
Career mentors, 100
CareerOneStop, 31
Career planning, 108–112
  checklist, 110–111
  educational decisions and, 4
  evaluating, 108, 110
  formulating action plan, 112
  personal factors in, 2–3
  tasks/steps involved in, 7–8
Change, and decision making, 60
Chronological résumé, 80. *See also* Résumé
  example of, 89f, 91f
College, 38
  reasons to attend, 39
Commitment, and career planning, 2
Common errors, in résumé, 80–81
Complex problem-solving skills, 17
Compromise, and career planning, 2
Computerized résumé packages, 82

Construction occupations, 72
Contacts, for job search
  direct, 100
  personal, 100
Control, of decision making, 61
Conventional interests, 14t
  and associated skills, 19t
  and work values, 16t
Conventional (organizer) personality type, 11
Co-operative experiences, 52
Cover letters, 94–97
  e-mail, 95, 97f
  examples of, 94f, 95f, 96f, 97f
Curriculum, undergraduate, 40–41
Cyber-interviews, 104. *See also* Job interview

D

Decision making
  change and, 60
  control and, 61
  dimensions of, 56, 56f
  goals and, 61–63
  obstacles in, 60
  personal style of, 58–59, 59f
  process, 61–67
  review, 66–67
  risk taking and, 57–58
  values, 56–57
Decision-Making Style Inventory (DMSI), 59f
Decision situation, 59
Demographic patterns, and workplace, 69
Department of Labor. *See* U.S. Department of Labor
Developmental approach, 1–2
Direct contacts, 100
Direct experience, as a source of occupational information, 32
DISCOVER, 32
Distance learning, 51
DMSI. *See* Decision-Making Style Inventory (DMSI)

E

Education
  choices, 37–39
  college, 39
  decision making, 39–40
  distance learning, 51
  experiential. *See* Experiential learning
  graduate degree, 38, 48–49
  major, choosing. *See* Major
  professional degree, 48–49
  on résumé, 83–84
  undergraduate curriculum, 40–41
Educational programs, 38
Educational Testing Service (ETS), 32
Electronic résumé, 82

E-mail, 104
  address on résumé, 83
  cover letter, 95, 97f
  networking contact letter, 99f
  résumé by, 82
Employment projections, 71–74
Employment services, and job search, 99
Enterprising interests, 14t
  and associated skills, 19t
  and work values, 16t
Enterprising (persuader) personality type, 11
Environmental factors, and career
    choice, 20–24
Errors, in résumé, 80–81
Etiquette, in job interview, 104
ETS. *See* Educational Testing Service (ETS)
Experiential learning. *See also* Education
  co-operative experiences, 52
  extracurricular activities, 51
  internships, 51–52
  service learning, 52
  study-abroad, 52
  volunteer work, 52
  work experiences, 51
External decision maker, 58
Extraction occupations, 71
Extracurricular activities, 51

F

Fair Employment Practices Act, 105
Family
  and career choice, 20–22
  job leads and, 100
Farming, as occupation, 72
Financial operation, as occupation, 72
Firsthand experience, as a source of occupational information, 32
Fishing, as occupation, 72
Flowchart, to career decision, 109f
FOCUS V.2, 32
Forestry, as occupation, 71
Formats
  of job interview, 103
  of résumé, 80
Friends, job leads and, 100
Functional résumé, 80, 84, 85. *See also* Résumé
  example of, 90f

G

Gender, and career choice, 23
Genogram, career, 20–23
Globalization, and workplace, 69
Goals
  decision-making process and, 61
  on résumé, 83

Graduate degree, 38, 48–49
Green jobs, 70
Group interview, 103
Guidance systems, 32
Guide for Occupational Exploration, 14

H

Hidden market, 99
Holland, John
   interest inventories of, 12
   personality types of, 11–12
Holland Occupational Interest Areas, 14t
   and work values, 16t

I

Illegal inquiries, 105
Immigration, and workforce, 71
Indecision, 60
Informational interviews, 32–35
Information collection, in decision making process, 63
Installation/maintenance/repair occupation, 72
Interests, 12–14, 14t, 16t
   assessment of, 12–14
   change in, 12
   concept of, 12
   in occupational selection, 12
Internal decision maker, 58
Internet, 28–31
   job search on, 100–101
Internship, 51–52
Interviews
   academic major, 46–48
   informational, 32–35
   job. *See* Job interview
Investigative interests, 14t
   and associated skills, 19t
   and work values, 16t
Investigative (thinker) personality type, 11

J

Job fairs, 100
Job interview
   appearance, 104
   cyber-interview, 104
   etiquette in, 104
   follow-up, 104–105
   formats of, 103
   preparing for, 101–102
   purpose of, 101
   rejection, dealing with, 105–106
   types of, 103
Job leads, 98–99. *See also* Job search

Job search
   action steps in, 78–79
   cover letters and, 94–97
   on Internet, 100–101
   rejection, dealing with, 105–106
   review, 106
   sources of, 99–100

K

Krumboltz, John, 20

L

Learning, experiential. *See also* Education
   co-operative experiences, 52
   extracurricular activities, 51
   internships, 51–52
   service learning, 52
   study-abroad, 52
   volunteer work, 52
   work experiences, 51
Legal inquiries, 105
Life skills, 74–75

M

Major
   academic interview, 46–48
   choosing, 41–45
   and interests, 42–45
   researching, 46–48
Management, as occupation, 72
Material moving occupations, 72
Mentors, 100
Mentors, career, 100
Motivation, and career planning, 2

N

Name, on résumé, 83
Networking, and job search, 99
Newspapers, and job search, 99

O

Obstacles, in decision-making situations, 60
Occupational groups, 72, 73f
Occupational information
   career guidance system, 32
   informational interviews, 32–35
   Internet and, 28–31
   O*NET, 28–31
   overview, 26
   sources of, 28–35

Occupational Information Network. *See* O*NET
  (Occupational Information Network)
Occupational Outlook Handbook, 31, 49, 73
  fastest growing occupations, 50t–51t, 71f
Occupations. *See also* specific occupation
  fastest growing, 49t–50t, 71f
  with numerical job growth, 49t–50t
Office and administrative support occupations, 72
O*NET (Occupational Information Network),
  12, 28–31

P

Personal data, on résumé, 86
Personality
  and career choice, 11
  Holland's types, 11–12
Personal style of decision making, 58–59
  defined, 58
  spontaneous, 58, 59
  systematic, 58, 59
Problem, defining, 61
Production occupations, 72
Professional and related occupations, 72
Professional degree, 48–49

Q

Qualifications summary, on résumé, 83

R

Realistic (doer) personality type, 11
Realistic interests, 14t
  and associated skills, 19t
  and work values, 16t
References, on résumé, 86
Rejection, dealing with, 105–106
Resource management skills, 17
Responsibility, and career planning, 2
Résumé
  appearance, 81–82
  common errors, 80–81
  cover letters with. *See* Cover letters
  dissemination, 82–83
  electronic, 82
  formats, 80
  maintaining, 83–88
  sample, 88f–93f
  scannable, 82–83
  video, 82
Review
  decision making, 66–67

Review, job search, 106
Risks, and decision making, 57–58

S

Sales and related occupations, 72
Scannable résumé, 82–83
Service learning, 52
Service occupations, 72
SES. *See* Socioeconomic status (SES)
SIGI 3, 32
Skills, 16–19
  basic, 17
  complex problem-solving, 17
  occupational interest areas and, 18, 19t
  resource management, 17
  on résumé, 85, 92f
  social, 17–18
  systems, 18
  technical, 18
Social (helper) personality type, 11
Social interests, 14t
  and associated skills, 19t
  and work values, 16t
Social skills, 17–18
Socioeconomic status (SES), 20
Software résumé packages, 82
Spontaneous decision maker, 58, 59
STAR Technique, 103
State Job Banks, 31
21st Century Skills, 74
Study-abroad programs, 52
Summer job résumé, 93f
Systematic decision maker, 58, 59
Systems skills, 18

T

Targeted interviewing approach, 103
Technical programs, 38, 40, 41
Technical skills, 18
Technological advances, and workplace, 69–70
Transportation occupations, 72

U

Undergraduate curriculum, 40–41
U.S. Bureau of Labor Statistics, 69, 71
U.S. Department of Labor, 70, 99
  educational programs, 38
  occupational groups classification, 72
  O*NET. *See* O*NET (Occupational Information Network)
  on skills, 16–18
  on work values, 14. *See also* Work, values
USAJOBS, 31

V

Values
  concept, 14
  decision making and, 56–57
  life, 14
  work, 14–16, 16t
Video résumé, 82
Vocational program, 38
Volunteer work, 52

W

Work
  concept of, 3–4
  values, 14–16, 16t

Work experiences, 51
  direct, 32
  on résumé, 84–85
Workforce trends, 70–71
Workplace
  demographic patterns and, 69
  factors influencing, 69–70
  globalization and, 69
  preparing, 74–75
  technological advances and, 69–70
  trends in, 70
Workshops, on interview, 102
World-of-Work Map, 32
Writing
  cover letters, 94–97, 94f, 95f, 96f, 97f
  résumé. *See* Résumé